MW00848542

Destined For Dominion

By A.L. Gill

Published By
Powerhouse Publishing
P.O. Box 99
Fawnskin, CA 92333

Books by A.L. and Joyce Gill

God's Promises for Your Every Need
Out! In the Name of Jesus
Victory Over Deception!

Manuals by A.L. and Joyce Gill

Authority of the Believer
How to Quit Losing and Start Winning

The Church Triumphant
Through the Book of Acts

God's Provision for Healing
Receiving and Ministering God's Healing Power

Supernatural Living
Through the Gifts of the Holy Spirit

Ministry Gifts
Apostles, Prophets, Evangelists, Pastors, Teachers

New Creation Image
Knowing Who You Are in Christ

Praise and Worship
Becoming Worshipers of God

Destined For Dominion, Revised – 1992
Copyright @ 1987– First Edition 1988
As Not Made For Defeat!
Printed in The United States of America
All Rights Reserved
ISBN 0-941975-12-6

Foreword by Dr. Gary L. Greenwald

From the opening illustration in Chapter One on **The Invisible War** to the closing scripture in **The Church Triumphant,** this incredible book explodes with scriptural teachings and first-hand, true accounts of everyday spiritual warfare.

A.L. and Joyce Gill have traveled throughout the nations equipping believers and transfroming them from spiritual wimps into God-anointed warriors. Whereas Frank Peretti, in **This Present Darkness** peaked our interest in our spiritual battles with satan's dark forces, A.L. Gill takes us on into real life training and victorious encounters with the enemy.

Personally, I can highly recommend **Destined For Dominion** because of my close friendship with A.L. and Joyce Gill. I've observed their supernatural ministry on several occasions where powerful miracles, healings, and the "strange acts of God" occurred. While some "gifted" ministries tend to become "spooky spiritual," the Gills are always loving, humorous, down to earth, and sincerely caring about people. Their heart's cry is to prepare every believer, small and great, for spiritual victories in their daily lives.

As you read these anointed pages, your faith will soar and your heart will boldly declare, "I'm more than a conqueror and I'm destined for dominion!"

Pastor, Eagle's Nest Ministries

Poetic Summary by Dr. T.L. Osborn

The book, **Destined For Dominion**, provides fresh enlightenment and scriptural knowledge for believers. It gives them the reason for believing. It will help readers in the practical application of their faith. I believe A.L. Gill has made a valuable contribution to the church through this book. I thought it might be nice to summarize the essence of its contents in a poem.

DESTINED FOR DOMINION

God's dream for human persons
Is total and complete.
We're created in His image,
And never for defeat.
But Lucifer, our enemy
Was poisoned by conceit;
Jealous of God's glory,
He was sentenced to defeat.
The battle was invisible;
Satan was cast out.
So he came to God's creation
And sowed his seed of doubt.
Instead of life, death was our lot;
T'was the wages of our sin.
But Jesus came and paid the price
So our new life could begin.
We're now a new creation;
Our rights have been restored.
Look out, Satan! Here we come!
We're empowered by God's Word.
The blood of Jesus covers all.
We live and move in Him.
We speak His Word. We use His Name.
His Presence makes us win.
When God formed us in His image,
His species to repeat,
We were **Destined For Dominion,**
And never for defeat.

Table of Contents

Chapter One
The Invisible War   7

Chapter Two
The Eternal Rebellion   19

Chapter Three
Then Came Jesus!   31

Chapter Four
From the Cross to the Throne   47

Chapter Five
Authority Restored   59

Chapter Six
Look Out Satan, Here Comes the Church!   73

Chapter Seven
There's Power in the Blood   91

Chapter Eight
God's Word, Alive and Powerful!   103

Chapter Nine
Speak the Word Only   119

Chapter Ten
The Name Above Every Name   137

Chapter Eleven
Jesus, The Authority of His Name   153

Chapter Twelve
The Church Triumphant   173

Chapter One

The Invisible War

It was a perfect winter evening in Southern California when we parked our car in front of the big house in Anaheim Hills. As I turned off the engine, the sun was going down, silhouetting the beautiful house at the end of the cul-de-sac.

"That's our new house; we've just bought it," I announced to my parents, who were sitting in the back seat of the car. They had arrived from Houston a few hours earlier and this was the first time they had seen the house.

To our right, we could see a breathtaking, panoramic view that included the valley and beautiful snow-capped mountains in the distance. The lights from the houses and cars below sparkled like diamonds and rubies.

We had been talking about the events of the previous months. My wife, Joyce, and I were telling my mom and dad how God had led us to buy this house, how He had confirmed it in so many ways that there could be no doubt.

The escrow had closed a few days before and now the house was legally ours. However, a family was living there and they refused to move. They had moved into the house about six months before on a lease-option to buy. After making their first monthly payment, they were deceived into believing God had given them the house. Since "it was theirs," they had refused to make any more payments to the previous owner or to move out.

When I signed the contract to purchase the house, I had assumed this matter would be taken care of long before the escrow closed. The previous owner had been very frustrated with the slow moving legal notices and eviction proceedings.

Now the escrow had closed and it was my problem. I was considering the best method to force the people out of my house. The time was short. Since Joyce and I were to leave on a missionary trip to Hong Kong and the Philippines in two weeks, it was important to be moved in and to have the children settled in their new schools before that time.

My first option was simply to explain the situation to the family, telling them the house had been sold, and that we needed to move in the following weekend. My second option was to hire a lawyer. I knew that if they persisted in their decision to stay in the house, it would take about three months of unpleasant proceedings to move them out legally.

We have found that usually when the Lord reveals a new dimension of truth, we soon have an opportunity to prove that truth in our lives. While we were in the process of purchasing the house, God had begun to teach us about the authority we have in Jesus Christ.

The Lord said this was a battle in the spirit world, and we weren't to say one word to the people. He reminded us that *we do not wrestle against flesh and blood, but against principalities, against powers, against the rulers of the darkness of this age, against spiritual hosts of wickedness in the heavenly places (Ephesians 6:12).* Our warfare wasn't with these people, but with the demonic force that was deceiving them, and thus hindering us from enjoying all that was rightfully ours.

To my own natural mind, this approach didn't seem logical. I wanted to take immediate action, but God had spoken to my spirit and I knew I must wait.

While the four of us sat in the car in front of the house that winter evening, talking about the location of various rooms and about the situation we were facing with the tenants, I noticed the front porch light was on.

Suddenly, God gave me the name of the leading spirit of deception that was causing the problems. I exclaimed, "Praise God! Satan, I bind you, in the name of Jesus! You spirits of deception, I bind you and I break your assignment over this house and everything you have tried to do to prevent us from taking possession of it."

Instantly, I was in the middle of a battle in the spirit realm over the house. I found myself speaking rapidly with authority to those demonic spirits. The moment I began to speak to the leading spirit of deception, the front porch light began to flash on and off. At first, I thought a child was flipping the light switch, and then I realized it would be impossible for anyone to flip a switch that fast. It was a manifestation of the spiritual warfare that was taking place over the house.

"All spirits of deception, I command you to leave in the name of Jesus!"

Joyce and my parents joined me in the warfare. We began to declare Scripture to the evil spirits.

And they overcame him by the blood of the Lamb and by the word of their testimony...

And these signs will follow those who believe: In My name they will cast out demons...

Behold, I give you the authority to trample on serpents and scorpions, and over all the power of the enemy... (Revelation 12:11, Mark 16:17, Luke 10:19)

All this time the front porch light continued to flash violently. We began to laugh at the antics of Satan with the confident joy that comes with seeing him defeated. We continued to speak the Word of God, to take dominion over demonic spirits and to order them to leave. After several minutes, we felt a release in our spirits and began to thank God for the victory. At that very moment, the light stopped flashing.

Our faith, confidence, and spiritual boldness grew when we saw the reality of this experience confirmed by the following events of the week.

The battle had been won! On the very next day, the people started looking for another house. They found another place and when we arrived with our furniture on the following Saturday, the house was empty, swept clean, ready for us and our furniture. We had not spoken one word to them.

The battle had been won, not with the weapons of the flesh, not by legal recourse, but with spiritual weapons that are ...*mighty in God for pulling down strongholds* (2 Corinthians 10:4).

We began to realize that for much of our lives, we had been fighting the wrong enemies. We had been fighting other people, those Paul referred to as "flesh and blood." We had been fighting with the wrong weapons, our human, carnal ones. We thought back over our lives, how time after time we were defeated, frustrated and even driven to the point of physical exhaustion trying to win the battles of life.

Now, when battles come against us, we think back to that beautiful winter evening when we sat in front of our new home in California and saw Satan defeated by the mighty spiritual weapons God had given us. We remember the exhilaration and joy of seeing Satan defeated when we walked in the reality of God's Word. We realize again, *The weapons of our warfare are not carnal but mighty in God for pulling down strongholds (2 Corinthians 10:4).*

If unseen spirit-beings are our real enemies; if it's in the realm of the spirit, and not in the realm of the flesh, in which the real battle is to be won, we should search the Scriptures diligently to discover who our real enemies are.

Who are the enemies described in Ephesians as principalities, powers, rulers of the darkness of this age and spiritual hosts of wickedness in the heavenly places *(Ephesians 6:12)?*

Why are these enemies so intent on destroying us? What are they trying to accomplish? How do they function? How did this all begin?

Peter warns us, *Be sober, be vigilant; because your adversary the devil walks about like a roaring lion, seeking whom he may devour (1 Peter 5:8).* The

11

devil is our real enemy, so these spirit-beings we are wrestling with must be working with him.

Why is it that we, earthly human beings, are in a conflict with something, or someone, we can't see?

I began to search the Scripture for the answers to these challenging questions and God revealed to me some fascinating, exciting truths about our part in the warfare between God and Satan.

As God began to take me back through the pages of eternal history, I knew there was never a time that God didn't exist. When He created the vast universe, He created spirit-beings called angels who would carry out His directives to keep the universe moving in perfect harmony with His will.

The apostle Paul wrote, *For by Him all things were created that are in heaven and that are on earth, visible and invisible, whether thrones or dominions or principalities or powers. All things were created through Him and for Him. And He is before all things, and in Him all things consist (Colossians 1:16,17).*

These spirit-beings, or angels, were organized with definite functions and a definite chain of command. They were identified as archangels, cherubims, seraphims, principalities, powers, thrones and dominions. Above all this angelic throng, God had placed a magnificent being to rule and govern in His name. He was called the "Star of the Morning" and his name was Lucifer.

Everywhere in the universe, millions of angels were busy as they joyfully carried out their responsibilities. The focal point of the entire creation was the throne of God where the angels gathered to praise and worship Him.

The beauty of the throne room was beyond description and even beyond our imagination. The sparkling of millions of colorful, precious jewels must have reflected the overwhelming light that radiated from the glory of the presence of God. There was an excited hum of activity as the angels surrounded the throne, coming and going on numerous assignments.

The atmosphere was electrified with the power of God's presence. Even angels were unable to remain on their feet, but were joyfully bowing in praise and worship. The glory of the light of God's love that permeates heaven was exhilarating beyond description.

The sounds of glorious, beautiful music mingled with thousands of voices in waves of praise and worship to the Lord. Exclamations of "Holy, Holy" and "Worthy is the Lamb" mingled with joyful "Hallelujahs" in the perfect harmony of the celestial orchestra.

As a person's eyes, dancing with the excitement of this marvelous scene, gradually adjusted to the glorious light streaming from the throne of God, they would begin to distinguish other objects that surrounded the presence of God.

In the place of highest honor stood Lucifer, the most beautiful of God's creations. His wings covered, or overshadowed, the throne of God, like the golden cherubims in the earthly tabernacle that covered the mercy seat in the Holy of Holies. He's described in Ezekiel as *the full measure and pattern of exactness*

— giving the finishing touch to all that constitutes completeness — full of wisdom and perfect in beauty. You were the anointed cherub that covers with overshadowing [wings] (Ezekiel 28:12,14a Amplified Bible).
He was entrusted as a guard, or protector, of the throne of God. Even his name, Lucifer, was descriptive of the glorious light of God's presence that was reflected through his beauty. He was known as the "Star of the Morning" because his brilliance wasn't obscured, even by the intense light that radiated from God.

His voice could be heard above the other angels, as he led them in praise and worship to God. The great sounds that came from his throat sounded like timbrels, drums and tambourines, stringed instruments, pipes and flutes *(Ezekiel 28:13, Isaiah 14:11)*.

His function, in this place of highest honor and authority, was to receive commands directly from God and then to direct God's angelic creation. His directions were passed down through the chain of command to the cherubims, seraphims, living creatures, thrones, dominions, principalities, authorities and powers. Millions of angels moved in perfect harmony with God's will.

Then, suddenly, on one unforgettable and regrettable day, for the first time, all the beauty and harmony of heaven was shattered. It began with a thought in Lucifer's mind. For a split second, his thoughts turned from God to himself. He noticed his own beauty and thought of his own importance. God said, *Your heart was lifted up because of your beauty;*

you corrupted your wisdom for the sake of your splendor (Ezekiel 28:17a).

Instead of rejecting that thought, instead of casting down the imagination that exalted itself against his knowledge of God, he allowed it to continue. In the glistening, transparent gold of heaven's throne room, he allowed his eyes to continue to gaze at his own reflected beauty. He found himself experiencing a totally new emotion — pride. He turned his head and body for another gaze in the heavenly mirror. "It is true," he thought, "I am the most beautiful creature throughout the universe."

His beautiful voice, seconds before raised in praise and worship to God, had drifted off and was now silent. His thoughts jumped to his own position of importance. Why should he continue to direct all the praise and worship to God? Wouldn't it be fitting to keep some for himself?

His thoughts raced forward, as he glanced at his own beautiful image. "Why should I share this glory with God?" Rebellion leaped up in his heart. "I will exalt my throne above God's. I will ascend. Yes, I will make myself like the most High God *(Isaiah 14:13,14).* Surely, I can entice the angels into following me; they have always followed my directions without question."

Lucifer had committed high treason in the courts of heaven. He had rebelled against the Almighty One of the universe, the God who had created him and entrusted him to the place of highest honor.

Lucifer had made a serious miscalculation. He wasn't able to deceive all the angels of God. There was dissension in the angelic ranks. The angels under the command of Gabriel and Michael remained with unflinching faithfulness to God.

However, a third of the principalities, powers, thrones and dominions were deceived and followed their leader, Lucifer, in his rebellion. The Word of God reveals, *His tail drew a third of the stars* (angels) *of heaven and threw them to the earth (Revelation 12:4a).*

The apostle John wrote about when Satan and his angels were cast out of heaven. *And war broke out in heaven: Michael and his angels fought against the dragon; and the dragon and his angels fought, But they did not prevail, nor was a place found for them in heaven any longer. So the great dragon was cast out, that serpent of old, called the Devil and Satan, who deceives the whole world; he was cast to the earth, and his angels were cast out with him. Then I heard a loud voice saying in heaven, "Now salvation, and strength, and the kingdom of our God, and the power of His Christ have come, for the accuser of our brethren, who accused them before our God day and night, has been cast down (Revelation 12:7-10)."*

Because of Satan's sin of rebellion, he was cast out of heaven. *Thus says the Lord God: "By the abundance of your trading you became filled with violence within, and you sinned; therefore I cast you as a profane thing out of the mountain of God; and I destroyed you, O covering cherub, from the midst of the fiery stones (Ezekiel 28:12b,16)."*

Perhaps, only those who have felt the pain and hurt of being rejected and betrayed by their closest friend can begin to understand how God must have felt at that time. He had loved Lucifer and trusted him with great responsibilities in heaven. When Lucifer and the angels had stood before Him through the ages of eternity and had sung songs of praise and worship, His perfect love had flowed out to them in great and overwhelming measure.

How it must have hurt God to see the ones He loved so dearly, turn their backs in rebellion toward Him. His perfect love desired to forgive, but His perfect righteousness couldn't co-exist with rebellion and sin. His perfect justice must be carried out. Lucifer and his rebellious angels must be expelled from heaven.

Chapter Two

The Eternal Rebellion

All the universe was beautiful and perfect. There was no place of judgment and punishment prepared for Lucifer and his followers. Before this time, there had been no need.

As God searched the vast universe for a place, His attention was drawn to an insignificant planet in a small solar system. Here, Satan and his demonic forces would await the final judgment. God, in great sorrow, would prepare a burning lake of fire as the place of confinement for them throughout eternity. However, first, on earth, God would prove His perfect justice and judgment of Satan and his demons for all creation to see. It was on this planet that Satan was to be totally defeated.

At God's command, His faithful angels, led by the archangel, Michael, waged war against Satan and his rebellious followers. They were no match for God's angelic host and were cast from heaven down to planet earth.

It had all happened so quickly. Just moments before, these two opposing forces had been closest friends and fellow worshipers around the throne of God.

Now, it was like they had never known them. Their heavenly names were taken away. Lucifer, the anointed cherub, the highest angel, had become

Satan, the accuser. Their nature had totally changed. Their love had immediately changed to hate, their faithfulness to rebellion. Their voices of praise were now uttering curses. Their radiant countenances were replaced with vile darkness.

When Satan and his demon followers arrived on earth, they were seething with anger and humiliation from their defeat. The last thing they wanted to see was anything that reminded them of God. And yet, they found themselves on a planet God had created.

The Bible begins with these words, *In the beginning God created the heavens and the earth (Genesis 1:1).* When God created this earth, He did not create it empty and void. He created it to be inhabited. Isaiah reveals God's purpose in creating the earth when He wrote, *For thus says the LORD, Who created the heavens, Who is God, Who formed the earth and made it, Who has established it, Who did not create it in vain* (empty), *Who formed it to be inhabited (Isaiah 45:18a).*

There may have been beautiful mountains, valleys, lakes, green trees, meadows covered with flowers, and all types of creatures living in perfect harmony.

Lucifer had become Satan, the destroyer. His face was flushed with vehement hate and anger. As reported in the book of John, he had come as a thief *to steal, and to kill, and to destroy (John 10:10a).*

In Genesis 1:2a we read, *The earth was without form, and void; and darkness was on the face of the deep.* The earth may have become without form and void, sometime after it was created to be inhabited. Perhaps the destruction that caused the earth to be *without form and void* was caused by a judgment of God upon it due to Satan's rebellion.

The destruction could have been caused by Satan's earthshaking temper tantrums wreaking havoc with the beauty of the earth. Perhaps, this was the destruction described by Jeremiah, *I beheld the earth, and indeed it was without form, and void; and the heavens, they had no light. I beheld the mountains, and indeed they trembled, and all the hills moved back and forth. I beheld, and indeed there was no man, and all the birds of the heavens had fled (Jeremiah 4:23-25).*

Now demolished, ruined and void, the earth was a suitable home for the one who came to kill, steal and destroy. Everything Satan touched was destroyed.

In the devil's twisted mind, he may have thought he could strike back and in some way get even with the Creator by destroying His creation. Satan's hatred for God had warped his judgment. His pride had made him want to be the pre-eminent ruler. Now, the only world Satan had to rule was empty and void.

The Bible is not clear regarding the exact sequence of these events. However, we do know that it was on this earth that Lucifer and his angels were cast after their rebellion in heaven. Lucifer, the anointed of God became known as Satan or "the devil." His angels, after their fall, became known as demons.

Instead of the glorious sounds of praise and music, there was despair and silence. Instead of the glorious light of God's presence, Satan and his fallen angels were now in total darkness. Was this the end? Was Satan trapped in desolation and darkness for all eternity?

God had a plan. Satan's defeat wasn't yet complete. The Bible doesn't say, but possibly eons of time had passed with Satan and his followers trapped in total darkness and silence. Suddenly, a sound was heard. It may have sounded like the rushing, mighty wind described in the book of Acts. It was the Spirit of God moving upon the face of the waters.

Panic must have gripped the heart of Satan and his followers. "No! It couldn't be. Surely God wasn't coming to this planet!" But, He was.

The voice of God boomed throughout the universe, *Let there be light! (Genesis 1:3)* and immediately light appeared.

What was going on? There must have been great confusion in Satan's ranks. Their hearts must have still been beating in fear, when on the next day, the voice of God was heard again, and then again, and again, day after day.

All that Satan had destroyed was being recreated! Dry land appeared, then beautiful vegetation and trees, birds and fish, along with cattle and all species of beautiful animals. Before Satan knew what was happening, he was surrounded by a beautiful, recreated earth.

How humiliating it must have been for Satan to have God come to earth and demonstrate His creative power again. His anger grew stronger every day. "God should leave me alone," he screamed.

By the fifth day, the recreation was complete. Perhaps Satan thought God would leave him and his earth alone. After all, God had a whole universe to run. Why would He take so much interest in one insignificant planet?

Then, on the sixth day the voice of God was heard to say, *Let Us make man in Our image (Genesis 1:26a)!* God knelt down to the ground and began to form a figure with His hands. He created it from the dust of the ground.

Peering curiously over God's shoulder, Satan watched as God shaped and molded this thing called a man. What was this new thing to be? What would it look like? Suddenly in shocked horror, Satan jumped back as he exclaimed, "No! No! It can't be! This creature looks just like God!" Was God making a creation that looked just like Himself to live on planet earth? How awful! Satan couldn't believe his eyes.

Now, what was God doing?

Perhaps God picked up this limp, lifeless form, and held it in front of Himself. It must have looked like a mirror reflection of God. He put his arms around the new creation, held it close to His own body, eye to eye, nose to nose, and mouth to mouth. Then God *breathed into his nostrils the breath of life; and man became a living being (Genesis 2:7)*. Adam sprang to life with the very breath and life of God within him.

Desperate panic gripped the heart of Satan. This new creature looked just like God! He walked like God! He talked like God! He acted like God in every way! He was made in God's image!

Soon, God put Adam to sleep, took one of his ribs and formed another one of these God-like creatures, a woman. *Then God blessed them, and God said to them, "Be fruitful and multiply; fill the earth and subdue it (Genesis 1:28a)."*

Satan cringed in horror. Human beings were to multiply and fill the earth. He could visualize the whole earth full of these God-like creatures. What an insult, an indignity; everywhere he and his demonic followers would look, they would see the images of God!

Then God spoke His first words regarding mankind, words that revealed His creative purpose for His newly created beings. *Let them have dominion (Genesis 1:26b)!* God spoke to His new creations, and said He had given all of the earth to them! They were to subdue the earth and to have dominion over every living thing that moved on the earth.

"No! No! No!" Satan gasped. God was literally making men and women the rulers of this world. God was giving them his kingdom on earth! He was giving everything to them. They were to have dominion over all of the works of God's hands on this planet.

The realization of what that meant stunned Satan. If Adam and Eve were to have dominion over everything that creeps upon the earth, that included him. It included all the demonic spirits. They were to have dominion over his kingdom on earth. They would rule him!

How humiliating to Satan! Everything written in Isaiah fourteen, that Satan had willed to be in his rebellion, was being given to mankind. Satan had declared: *I will ascend into heaven.* Now mankind had been created to live and reign with God forever. In the book of Revelation, John revealed, *they shall be priests of God and of Christ, and shall reign with Him* (Revelation 20:6b).

In his rebellion Satan had declared, *I will exalt my throne above the stars* (angels) *of God.* Paul wrote, *"Do you not know that we shall judge angels* (I Corinthians 6:3a)?

Satan boasted, *I will also sit on the mount of the congregation on the farthest sides of the north.* Paul wrote that God *raised us up together, and made us sit together in the heavenly places in Christ Jesus* (Ephesians 2:6).

Satan had said, *I will ascend above the heights of the clouds.*

The Word declares, *For the Lord Himself will descend from heaven with a shout, with the voice of an archangel, and with the trumpet of God. And the dead in Christ will rise first. Then we who are alive and remain shall be caught up together with them in the clouds to meet the Lord in the air. And thus we shall always be with the Lord* (I Thessalonians 4:16-17).

In his final and ultimate words of rebellion, Satan had declared, *I will be like the Most High.* However, to the horror of Satan, God said, *Let Us make man in Our image, according to Our likeness* (Genesis 1:26a).

All the hatred that Satan had toward God was now directed toward these God-like human beings. Satan stood trembling in apprehension and intense anger. It was obvious Adam and Eve were his enemies. Satan must find a way to steal this dominion from them. They must be destroyed!

On the seventh day God rested; His work was complete. It was perfect. There was nothing more to add. God took the day to enjoy the beauty of the works of His hands.

God's love for Adam and Eve was more evident each day. He created a beautiful garden where they were to live and every evening He came down and talked and fellowshipped with them.

Adam's great intelligence and wisdom were demonstrated as he gave names to all the animals on the earth. He used his dominion when he lovingly directed the affairs of the entire earth. All the animals were living in perfect harmony with one another. It was a paradise of beauty, love and harmony.

God hadn't created Adam a mindless robot. He had given him free volition. Adam willfully and joyfully served and fellowshipped with God. He was faithful in his administrative duties over the entire earth. Eve was lovingly at his side, supporting and helping him in his responsibilities. Together, they tended the garden that was full of beautiful trees, laden with choice fruit which were delicious to eat.

God had given Adam and Eve the freedom of choice. He told them they could eat from all the trees of the garden, but one. It was the tree of the knowledge of good and evil. He warned them not to eat the fruit of that tree, for if they did, they would die.

The fiendish mind of Satan had already been working on various plans to destroy Adam and Eve. His hatred for them grew stronger each day. When Satan heard God tell them about the tree of the knowledge of good and evil, his eyes widened. "That's it!" He exclaimed. "Deception! I will deceive them into disobeying God with that tree!"

Satan thought if he could beguile them into exercising their will against God, he could trick them into joining their wills with his own. They would join him in his eternal rebellion against God. If he could deceive them about this one thing, he could destroy them.

Satan had been able to deceive a third of the angels in heaven. He was a master at deception, and Adam and Eve had free choice. The decision would be theirs! "I will quote what God said," he thought, "but change it just enough to cause them to doubt the reasonableness of what God said about that tree."

His scheme was beginning to come together. Satan would make his deception convincing. He rehearsed over and over exactly how he would make his approach, exactly how he would word each lie. He must deceive Adam. He must convince him to choose against God. That was the only way he could rob Adam of his authority and dominion over this earth. Then Satan's kingdom would be restored. He would again become the god of this world, and all humanity would be at his mercy.

As the rulers of this world, Adam and Eve had knowledge of all that was good. What need did they have for a knowledge of evil?

Satan wanted to walk into the Garden of Eden and begin his plan of deception, but now he had no authority to go anywhere or do anything on this earth. God had given this authority and dominion to Adam.

If Adam recognized Satan as God's enemy and exercised his dominion over him, he would have to flee.

So, Satan disguised himself as one of the beings that belonged in the garden. On that regrettable day, all of Satan's forces watched with hateful anticipation as Satan entered the Garden of Eden in the form of a serpent.

Satan's strategy went exactly as he had planned. Adam failed to exercise his dominion. Satan's carefully rehearsed deception worked. Eve took the fruit and ate it, and then gave it to Adam who was with her, and he also ate the forbidden fruit *(Genesis 3:6)*.

Adam was willfully deceived. He disobeyed God and surrendered to Satan his authority and dominion over this earth. He had been robbed! All humanity had been robbed! Satan was again the god of this world.

Satan and his demonic forces danced with glee. Adam and Eve were defeated. Through sin, their fellowship with God was broken. They were now slaves to Satan and his demonic forces.

How it must have delighted Satan to see Adam and Eve, the former rulers of this earth, hiding in shame behind a bush when God came that evening to fellowship with them. Now, instead of boldly walking in their God-given dominion authority, they were cowering in fear, guilt and condemnation.

Even as desperate as everything was at that moment, God still had a plan. Satan had won the battle, but the war wasn't over. God had a plan of redemption for men and women.

God spoke directly to Satan, who was still in the serpent's body, saying, *And I will put enmity between you and the woman, and between your seed and her Seed; He shall bruise your head, and you shall bruise his heel (Genesis 3:15).*

Satan didn't know that when God spoke of the seed of the woman, He was referring to the incarnate birth of Jesus. God's Son was going to come to this planet, born of a woman, and He was going to bruise Satan's head under His foot!

The battle Satan thought he had won was just beginning. God had a plan for his defeat.

Instead of going back joyfully to report his victory to the demonic forces, Satan was subdued while he pondered God's words to him. Who was this seed of the woman that God spoke about? What was God's plan to defeat him?

The eternal rebellion was to go on. Satan was helpless to strike back directly at God, so he would turn his whole hateful attention toward humanity.

As the number of inhabitants of the world increased, rulers of the darkness of the world would be assigned to every nation and organization. Principalities and powers would be assigned to oppress, and when an opening was found, even to possess men, women and children wherever and whenever possible.

Their job was to put people in bondage, to do everything possible to destroy them and to destroy their ability to communicate with God.

Satan was determined that the seed of a woman would never come to bruise his head.

Chapter Three

Then Came Jesus!

Satan thought back to the time in heaven when the conflict had begun. Everything had changed so quickly! He had desired to be like the Most High God! He had wanted to exalt himself above the throne of God. His desire was to be the supreme god of the whole universe.

One small planet in the universe seemed so insignificant in comparison to his original rebellious desire to rule the entire universe, but at least he owned it. The earth belonged to him. Now, he was a god. His pride soared as he repeated his newly gained titles repeatedly, "God of this World, Prince of the Power of the Air, Ruler of the Darkness of this Age!"

It was really true; all the kingdoms of this world belonged to him. Adam had surrendered to him his God-given authority over the earth.

For about four thousand years, Satan enjoyed his acquired titles and position. He enjoyed seeing men and women in sickness, pain, sorrow and poverty. People were living and dying in hopeless despair. Some were laying in the streets begging, their bodies crippled, dirty and gripped with pain. Many were blind, deaf and couldn't speak. Faces which had been created in the image of God were now disfigured, and parts of bodies were eaten away with leprosy.

Satan had held humanity under his control for thousands of years, and this was the result. Instead of men and women walking erect with boldness and confidence, they were bound by Satan and bowed down with crippling diseases. The demonic forces had done their work.

Even the spiritual leaders of that time had been deceived and robbed by Satan. All they had to offer humanity was a powerless, empty religion. They had become spiritually blind leaders of the blind.

The human race had been created in the image of God, but now because of sin, everywhere one looked, people were living in hopeless despair and demonic bondage.

God still had a plan! His love for the human race had never ceased. He remembered that beautiful day when He had created Adam from the dust of the ground. He remembered how He had lovingly taken that body up in His arms and embraced it, and breathed into Adam His own breath of life.

He remembered the wonderful times of fellowship when He would come down in the cool of the evening to be with Adam and Eve. As their loving heavenly Father, He longed to hold them again in His arms and breath into them His breath. It grieved Him to see His own children, whom He loved so dearly, living in despair. God hadn't forgotten His promise to Adam and Eve when He told Satan that the seed of the woman would bruise his head.

The apostle Paul wrote about God fulfilling this promise. *But when the fullness of the time had come, God sent forth His Son, born of a woman, born under the law, to redeem those who were under the law, that we might receive the adoption as sons (Galatians 4:4,5).*

Satan had invaded man's domain in the form and disguise of a serpent. Now when the fullness of time had come, God was going to invade Satan's domain as a man, in the form of a baby. The first Adam had lost his dominion for a time; the last Adam would regain it for eternity.

Even as unlovely as the human race in bondage to Satan's dominion of sin, sickness, poverty and death had become, God still loved men, women and children so much He sent His only Son to purchase their deliverance.

In the still of the night, on the hills near Bethlehem, an angel appeared to a group of shepherds with a message of great joy. *For there is born to you this day in the city of David a Savior, who is Christ the Lord (Luke 2:11).*

The angels that had come from heaven to announce this marvelous event couldn't contain their joy. While the shepherds watched, they burst forth with praise to God, singing in harmony, *Glory to God in the highest, and on earth peace, good will toward men (Luke 2:14)!*

God's plan was being fulfilled! The last Adam had arrived on planet earth. He was God's own Son. He had come so that the human race could be set free from the bondage of Satan and the dominion of his forces.

The promised seed of the woman had come, and as the angel had instructed Mary, His name was called Jesus! He had come to give life. The Son of God had come to destroy the works of the devil. Men, women and children were going to be set free from Satan's sickness, disease, poverty and death. For suffering, dying humanity, this was certainly *good tidings of great joy (Luke 2:10b)*.

Jesus was conceived by the Holy Ghost and born of a virgin. He was born without the sin nature, so He was without the curse that had been placed upon humanity. He was fully and completely man, as man was created to be, and yet fully and completely God in all of His undiminished deity.

The Son of God was qualified to pay the penalty for the sins of the human race. Since He was without sin, He did not carry the penalty of sin in His own life. The apostle Paul wrote, *For the wages of sin is death, but the gift of God is eternal life in Christ Jesus our Lord (Romans 6:23)*. Jesus, the Son of God, would die willingly on the cross to pay the penalty for sin.

Satan could never understand this love. In his depraved state, he couldn't even remember what love was. Satan and his followers lived only for themselves. They couldn't conceive of anyone leaving the wonders of heaven to become the sacrifice for poor, miserable, defeated humanity.

The joyful announcement of the host of angels to the shepherds outside Bethlehem brought desperate panic to Satan. "God's plan must be stopped! This baby must be killed!" Satan exclaimed to his forces. "How can we accomplish it?"

King Herod was the answer. Satan planted the thought in Herod's mind to kill all the babies under two years of age in the area of Bethlehem. Surely, this would include the Son of God.

This first attack against Jesus failed. An angel warned Joseph and Mary in a dream, and they escaped to Egypt with the infant Jesus. For thirty years, Satan waited for his opportunity to attack. The commotion on the banks of the Jordan River must have alarmed him. One called John the Baptist was preaching repentance and talking about the "kingdom of God."

"This earth is my kingdom," protested Satan to his demonic forces when they gathered beside the Jordan River to discover what was happening.

While they watched, the one called Jesus was baptized by John. When He came out of the water, the Holy Spirit of God descended like a dove upon Him. Suddenly, the voice of God the Father broke the silence as He exclaimed, *This is My beloved Son, in whom I am well pleased* (Matthew 3:17).

Satan must have seethed in anger at the sound of God's voice.

The earthly ministry of Jesus had just begun. But immediately, He was led by the Holy Spirit into the wilderness where He went without food for forty days.

Satan had been waiting for the right moment. Certainly, this was the time for his attack. Jesus would be very weak after going without eating for so long. Satan resorted to the weapon he had used so effectively down through the ages — deception. He had been able to deceive millions of angels. He had been able to deceive the first Adam using his desire for food. Why wouldn't it work on the last Adam?

He began his attack, *If You are the Son of God, command that these stones become bread (Matthew 4:3)*. Jesus was tempted, but instead of listening to Satan's deception, the Son of God quoted Scripture. *It is written,* He said, *Man shall not live by bread alone, but by every word that proceeds from the mouth of God (Matthew 4:4b)*.

Satan didn't give up easily. He had another plan. He would show Jesus how He could prove to all the world that He was the Son of God. He would show Jesus how to accomplish His goals.

He took Jesus to the highest point in Jerusalem, a point where everyone could see Him, and then he tempted Jesus to cast Himself down from the pinnacle of the temple. He assured Jesus that He wouldn't be hurt. The angels would lift Him up and all of the people watching, in and around Jerusalem, would know that Jesus was God.

Again, Jesus resisted him by quoting the Word, *You shall not tempt the Lord your God (Matthew 4:7b)*.

Then the devil took Jesus up into a high mountain, and showed Him all the kingdoms of this world. And he said unto Jesus, *All this authority I will give You, and their glory; for this has been delivered to me,* (by Adam); *and I give it to whomever I wish. Therefore, if You will worship before me, all will be Yours (Luke 4:6b, 7)*.

How paradoxical that Satan was offering to Jesus the kingdoms of the world. After all, in the beginning, Jesus had created the world. And God had given the authority over this planet to Adam. However, when Adam sinned, he willfully surrendered and delivered it to Satan. So Satan now had that right. He did have control of the kingdoms of this world.

How deceitful Satan was. He knew that Jesus had come to regain that dominion for the human race. Now, Satan offered Jesus the very thing He had come to earth to recover. If Jesus would only bow down and worship Satan, He could have the dominion back. Satan would return the authority over all of the kingdoms of this world to Him. Jesus could avoid the pain and agony of the cross. Jesus could restore the authority and dominion of the world to men and women. Jesus could go back to heaven and leave him alone!

Satan had conceived another one of his master plans of deceit. He was saying to Jesus, "Let's make a deal. I'll give you what you want! All I need is to be left alone."

But Jesus knew there was only one way to deal with the devil. First, He resisted him as He said, *"Away with you, Satan!"* Then, He went on to speak God's Word, *"For it is written, 'You shall worship the Lord your God, and Him only you shall serve (Matthew 4:10).'"*

Jesus was tempted in all points, even as man, yet without sin. He resisted Satan with the authority of the Word of God, and Satan had to leave.

Jesus returned, in the power of the Spirit, to Galilee. He had defeated Satan at his game of deception and now He was ready to begin His ministry of setting men free from Satan's dominion.

For thirty years, Jesus had seen children beside the roads begging in poverty. He had talked to men and women broken with discouragement and despair. He had watched the sick, the blind and those bruised with the hurts of this world. He had seen men, women and children held in slavery, as captives of Satan.

At the edge of town, Jesus had seen a man possessed by thousands of demons, running totally naked through the tombs. He had heard the lepers calling out their warning, "Unclean! Unclean!" and He had felt their desolation.

For thirty years, the Son of God had been surrounded by the unpleasantness of Satan's rule. He must have longed for the time of His ministry to begin. During the forty days in which Jesus fasted in the wilderness, His thoughts of love and compassion must have been reaching out to dying humanity.

Now was the time! He had been empowered with the Spirit of God when He was baptized in the Jordan River. He had won the victory over Satan's lies, deceit and temptations. For long years He had waited, but now His ministry was to begin.

Jesus returned to His home town of Nazareth, and went into the synagogue where He had spent time as a boy and young man. He opened the scroll to the book of Isaiah and began to read: *The Spirit of the Lord is upon Me, because He has anointed Me to preach the gospel to the poor. He has sent Me to heal the brokenhearted, to preach deliverance to the captives and recovery of sight to the blind, to set at liberty those who are oppressed, to preach the acceptable year of the Lord (Luke 4:18,19).*

The day had arrived. He was free to tell people the good news. Now, it was time to share the exciting news with His dearest friends. He read the prophecy that Isaiah had written about Him hundreds of years before.

The people couldn't believe their eyes and ears. They stared at Him in bewilderment. They wondered at the words He spoke. This couldn't be true. After all, this was Joseph's son. They had known him all his life. How could Jesus be the One sent to set the captives free?

Angry murmurs began to fill the synagogue. This carpenter's son was saying that He was the Messiah. That was blasphemy. He must be killed before this evil spread.

The message the people needed the most had been rejected.

Satan, still licking his wounds from his recent unsuccessful attempt to get Jesus to destroy Himself by jumping from the pinnacle of the temple, came on the scene. He put the thought into the minds of the angry people of Nazareth to take Jesus to the edge of the cliff by the city and to throw Him down headfirst.

Jesus escaped the mob at Nazareth and traveled to the city of Capernaum. Again, He went into the synagogue on the Sabbath day and taught the people, *And they were astonished at His teaching, for His word was with authority (Luke 4:32).*

In Capernaum, some of Satan's rebellious followers were living inside a man. He was apparently a religious man, since he had come to the synagogue, but he was possessed by unclean, lustful spirits. As

Jesus taught, the demons could stand it no longer. They began to cry out with a loud voice saying, *Let us alone! What have we to do with You, Jesus of Nazareth? Did You come to destroy us? I know You, who You are, — the Holy One of God (Luke 4:34)!*

They knew who Jesus was because in eternity past, before their rebellious fall from heaven, they had joined their voices in praise with the angels around the throne of God. They also knew why Jesus had come. They cried, *Did you come to destroy us?*

Jesus had come for that purpose. He was going to destroy the works of the devil. He rebuked the unclean demons and told them to come out of the man. They came out, and the man was instantly delivered.

The people were all amazed and began to say to one another, *What a word this is! For with authority and power He commands the unclean spirits, and they come out (Luke 4:36b).*

For four thousand years, Satan had ruled this world with authority and power. Now, here was a man, Jesus, speaking with authority and power and Satan's own demonic followers had to obey!

When Jesus left the synagogue, He went directly to Simon Peter's house where Peter's mother-in-law was sick with a very high fever. To the absolute amazement of those who heard, Jesus spoke with authority and power directly to the fever. He rebuked the fever. Peter's mother-in-law was instantly healed and started serving Jesus and the other guests.

This was only the beginning! For the next three years, everywhere Jesus went, people were set free from demonic forces and healed of all types of diseases. The works of Satan were being destroyed! The lame walked and the blind saw. The lepers were cleansed and healed. The demons were cast out, and the dead were raised. Jesus' disciples, and those who witnessed these miracles, were astounded at His authority.

Each time another person was healed or delivered, Satan would cringe in panic and humiliation. People were being loosed and set free from his demonic control and power. His kingdom was being destroyed. It was crumbling before his eyes. His anger and hatred for Jesus grew stronger every day. "Jesus must be stopped! But how?"

The people loved Jesus. For the first time, they were hearing words of encouragement and life. For the first time, there was hope. There was life instead of death, health instead of sickness, freedom instead of bondage. Truly, He was the King of kings and the Lord of lords. He was the Son of God. His kingdom was being established on the earth!

When Lazarus had been raised from the dead after being in the grave for four days, the news spread quickly.

Jesus was on His way into Jerusalem for the Feast of the Passover when the people ran into the streets and placed Him on a colt. They spread their coats on the roads in front of Him to make a royal welcome. The large crowd *began to rejoice and praise God with a loud voice for all the mighty works they had seen, saying: "Blessed is the King who comes in the name of the Lord! Peace in heaven and glory in the highest (Luke 19:37b,38)!"*

41

Satan could stand no more! Jesus must be stopped at all costs. For years, he had been working on plans to kill Jesus. "This world belongs to me! This is my kingdom! I took it from Adam and it's mine!" he would mutter to himself.

Now, men and women were exalting Jesus as King. They were still under Satan's dominion, but they were worshiping another.

Satan found the opening he needed. He deceived Judas and put a hideous thought into his mind. Judas would betray the Son of God.

Through the ages, God always had a plan of redemption. After Adam and Eve sinned, God provided animal sacrifices as an atonement, pointing forward to the redemptive work of Jesus on the cross. Satan deceived mankind into making these sacrifices an empty form of religion.

While Moses was in the mountains receiving the commandments of God, written by the hand of God, Satan was in the valley deceiving the people into worshiping a golden calf.

God had appointed priests. They were to be a special group, set apart to represent humanity to God and God to humanity. Through the beautiful symbolic design of the tabernacle, the temple and the sacrifices, God had revealed Himself and His redemptive plan for mankind.

Immediately, Satan had started a counterattack of deception and perversion. Satan had deceived the religious leaders, the men who according to God's plan were to be the spiritual leaders of the nation.

The deception was progressive. Over the years, a counterfeit religion took over God's wonderful plan. Men and women, again, lost their relationship with God. Religion, instead of revealing freedom through God's plan of redemption, placed them in an even greater bondage to the laws of men.

Now, Satan found no difficulty in deceiving the religious leaders into demanding Jesus' death. It was the religious leaders who led the crowd to cry out for His crucifixion. Shouts of, "Crucify Him! Crucify Him!" were heard in the streets.

Satan gloated with fiendish delight. There were a series of terrible events: the illegal trials, the whiplashing, the crown of thorns, the severe beatings, the mocking and spitting. It all took place so quickly one could hardly believe it was really happening to Jesus.

It appeared that hope was gone. The sounds of nails being driven into the hands and feet of the Son of God as He was nailed to the cross pierced, like daggers, into the hearts of those who heard it.

"It's happening! It's actually happening!" Satan shouted with an unholy delight that could be heard throughout the spirit world. "I have deceived men and women again. They are crucifying their Creator! I have them so deceived they are killing their only hope of salvation!"

"The world's mine. Jesus, the Son of God, has been defeated and I have used His God-like creation to do it!"

In a few hours, it would all be over. The demons joined in Satan's laughter as they prepared for the celebration of Jesus' death and total defeat.

But Satan, the master of deceit had deceived himself. He thought he was responsible for the death of Jesus. He didn't realize that Jesus, of His own free will, had given His life to redeem the human race.

Jesus, by His death, would bring about Satan's defeat. God's master plan of redemption would be carried out. Jesus would be the final Sacrifice.

It hadn't once entered the mind of Satan that it was he who was playing into God's hands of judgment. He was actually co-operating in and carrying out his own destruction. As prophesied after the fall of Adam and Eve, Satan had bruised Jesus' heel. He didn't realize that Jesus was preparing to crush his head! Satan didn't know that the prophecy given by God in the Garden of Eden was about to be fulfilled.

God had said, *I will put enmity between you and the woman, and between your seed and her Seed; He shall bruise your head, and you shall bruise His heel* (Genesis 3:15).

The Roman soldiers, the disciples and the people witnessing the crucifixion didn't know the tremendous battle going on in the spirit world.

Jesus took upon Himself the sin of all people, past, present and future. He became sin for us. The loving, heavenly Father couldn't look on sin and had to turn away from His Son. Feeling the awesome emptiness of the Father turning away, Jesus cried out, *My God, My God, why have You forsaken Me (Mark*

15:34b)? Jesus, the Son of God, who had always been one with the Father was now all alone.

Satan's elation at that moment was indescribable. He thought it would all be over when the Son of God died on the cross. He expected the angels would be forced to report a shameful, horrible defeat in the throne room of heaven.

The demonic forces were already jumping up and down in anticipation of total victory, when the words came from the lips of Jesus, *Father, into Your hands I commend My spirit (Luke 23:46b).*

Chapter Four

From the Cross to the Throne

It was complete!

Satan had been so intent on killing Jesus that he never realized the death of Jesus could free the human race from bondage. He didn't understand that the death of Jesus would redeem men and women from the slavery of sin.

When Jesus died, the penalty for sin had been paid. Jesus had taken upon Himself all our sins. He had become our substitute. Now these sins had to be borne away to the place of torments, to the darkness of the lowest pit in the depths of the earth. Here the perfect justice of God finally would be satisfied *(Psalms 88:1-7, Isaiah 53:4-11)*.

Jesus seemed helpless when He descended toward this place of torments. He was carrying a terrible burden — the sins of all the world.

The rich man, who had seen the beggar Lazarus resting in Abraham's bosom, was watching. The imprisoned spirits of unjust men and women who had rejected the message revealed in the Levitical sacrifices were watching. Now, the Lamb of God, the One they had rejected, was approaching.

Everywhere cries of anguish could be heard. Some joined with the rich man, begging for a drop of water to cool their tongues from the heat of the tormenting flames.

They were separated by a great gulf from those spirits in Paradise who, with Abraham and the other Old Testament saints, had believed God. How horrified these saints must have been to see the Son of God, covered with the filthiness of sin, descending into the darkest regions of the world.

Here on the brink of Hades, Satan had set up his headquarters. He hated humanity so much that he delighted in hearing their cries of torment. Satan didn't know that there awaited an even greater place of torments for him. He didn't know that God had already prepared for him and his demons an even hotter, burning lake of fire.

Satan, blinded by his driving hatred and desire to destroy the Son of God, was totally unaware of what was about to happen.

On a dismal hill outside the city of Jerusalem, the body of Jesus had gone limp in death as it hung on the cross. Immediately, the whole sky became dark. The earth began to shake and rocks came crashing down.

What violent upheaval in the spirit world was causing such destruction upon the surface of the earth?

In the temple, the thick veil that separated the Holy Place from the Holy of Holies, was torn from top to bottom. For hundreds of years, this veil had separated human beings from the earthly dwelling place of God so that they couldn't enter the presence of the Holy One.

Until this moment, only the high priest could enter the Holy of Holies behind the veil, and even then only once each year to take the blood offering from the sacrificial lamb and sprinkle it upon the mercy seat. Now, this veil was permanently torn asunder. Humanity was no longer separated from God. Through the death of the Son of God, men and women were given continuous, direct access to the presence of God.

Confusion was everywhere on the earth, under the earth, and in the spirit world. What was happening? What tremendous force in the unseen world was causing these violent upheavals and dramatic events on the surface of the earth?

When He hung on the cross, Jesus had taken upon Himself the sins of the world. He had become sin for us. The Father, who was perfect righteousness, couldn't look upon sin and had to turn His back on His own beloved Son. The perfect justice of God would be satisfied. The wrath of God was poured out upon Jesus, who of His own free will, had taken our sin and our punishment.

Now, Jesus, carrying this load of sin was approaching the place of torments, called Sheol in the Old Testament, or Hades in the New Testament. Here, Satan was holding the souls of unrighteous men captive, those he had deceived on earth, those who had rejected the message of salvation through the shed blood of the Lamb.

Satan was seething with hatred; he thought finally he had won. He delighted to see the intense agony and apparent helplessness of Jesus Christ, God's own Son.

Jesus had become the sacrificial Lamb. Now, even as the Levitical scapegoat, He was bearing our sins to a place where they would be remembered no more.

Satan must have danced with glee while he watched Jesus descending to the place where he had planned His eternal captivity and destruction. Here, Satan reigned as ruler of the darkness of the earth, and now, Jesus was his captive in those dark regions.

All the angels who had followed Satan in his rebellion must have gathered together to carry out this final act in the destruction of Jesus! The word had gone down through the ranks of the principalities, powers, rulers of the darkness of the world, and throughout all the spiritual wickedness in high places. They were all to be on hand to participate in this final act of rebellious hatred.

Acting on the commands from Satan's head-quarters of wickedness, they had all temporarily left their assigned posts upon the face of the earth. For four thousand years, they had carried out their instructions to kill, steal and destroy. Everywhere, human beings were demon-possessed, tormented and filled with hopeless diseases caused by the demonic spirits.

But now, the world could wait. The task at hand was too important to leave to a few demons. Jesus must be held captive and His body must be held in the grave.

This event was too great for any demon spirit to miss. The excitement of the moment was almost more than they could stand. It had happened at last! The Son of God would be destroyed!

This was the event that Isaiah had prophesied, *For He was cut off from the land of the living; for the transgressions of My people He was stricken. And they made His grave with the wicked — but with the rich at His death, because He had done no violence, nor was any deceit in His mouth (Isaiah 53:8b,9).*

Jesus' thoughts at this time were prophesied by David. *For my soul is full of troubles, And my life draws near to the grave.*

I am counted with those who go down to the pit; I am like a man who has no strength,

Adrift among the dead, Like the slain who lie in the grave, Whom You remember no more, And who are cut off from Your hand.

You have laid me in the lowest pit, In darkness, in the depths.

Your wrath lies heavy upon me, And You have afflicted me with all Your waves (Psalms 88:3-7).

In what seemed like the darkest hour of all eternity, Jesus entered Satan's kingdom of darkness, into the very center of Hades, and the "gates of hell" slammed shut behind Him.

Then it happened! At this moment of indescribable anguish, Jesus reached the bottom of the lowest pit in the place of torments. Falling to His knees, He dumped all the sins and iniquities of the entire world into that horrible abyss. The course of all eternity was changed when our sins were buried in the deepest part of the earth to be remembered no more.

Satan and his demons must have stood in stunned horror as they watched.

Jesus, a moment before, *like a man who has no strength,* had been doomed, in their eyes, to hopeless destruction. Suddenly, the power of God came upon Him. He sprang to His feet. His eyes were like a flame of fire when He turned and began to ascend from that pit. The "gates of Hades" could no longer contain the Son of God. They could no longer prevail against Him. In an explosion of power that shook the entire earth, the gates burst open. Jesus snatched the keys of death, hell and the grave from the hands of Satan as He stepped victoriously out of Hades.

Satan, in frightful confusion, ordered his counterattack. All the demonic forces were gathered in that great battle. Orders flashed down through the rank and file of his army. Desperate shouts, "Stop Him! Stop Him!" could be heard throughout the great host of the principalities, powers, rulers of the darkness, and spiritual wickedness in high places. They were all watching in horror as Jesus bound Satan. In those three days and three nights, Satan and his forces suffered their greatest defeat and humiliation.

Seven weeks later, on the Day of Pentecost, Peter preached a powerful sermon and led three thousand people to salvation. He knew what had happened to cause that resurrection! He told the people how, by their wicked hands, they had crucified Jesus of Nazareth. *Whom God raised up, having loosed the pains of death, because it was not possible that He should be held by it (Acts 2:24).*

Peter was quoting David when he continued, *Therefore my heart rejoiced, and my tongue was glad; moreover my flesh will also rest in hope, Because You will not leave my soul in Hades, nor will You allow Your Holy One to see corruption (Acts 2:26,27).*

He went on to explain, *He* (God) *would raise up the Christ to sit on his throne, he, foreseeing this, spoke concerning the resurrection of the Christ, that His soul was not left in Hades, nor did His flesh see corruption. This Jesus God has raised up, of which we are all witnesses (Acts 2:30b-32).*

Satan, in his blind rebellion, had underestimated the power of God. He had ignored the words of Jesus, *For as Jonah was three days and three nights in the belly of the great fish, so will the Son of Man be three days and three nights in the heart of the earth (Matthew 12:40).*

Jesus had outsmarted Satan! Indeed, He had entered the house of the strongman. Jesus bound the strongman, Satan, and then He spoiled Satan's goods and his house, just as He had taught His disciples to do.

Truly, *when the stronger than he comes upon him and overcomes him, he takes from him all his armor in which he trusted, and divides his spoils (Luke 11:22).*

The writer of the book of Hebrews wrote, *that by [going through] death He might bring to nought and make of no effect him who had the power of death, that is, the devil (Hebrews 2:14b Amplified Bible).*

Satan had been brought to nought. He had been rendered powerless and made of no effect. Satan, powerless, humiliated and disgraced, had to stand by helplessly and watch while his army was defeated. Jesus personally disarmed and spoiled all principalities and powers. This was the culmination of the work of Jesus on earth. John wrote, *For this purpose the Son of God was manifested, that He might destroy the works of the devil (1John 3:8b).*

At this time in the history of the world, when an army went out in battle against the army of another nation, the future of both nations was at stake.

The conquering army would enter the cities and take the riches of that nation. They would disarm the defeated soldiers, take them with their king, the king's family, prominent citizens and many other people, and strip off their clothing. They would bind them together in chains and march them in long columns behind the conquering general.

At home, the victorious nation would prepare a celebration for the returning general. They would build arches adorned with flowers along a special parade route. The citizens would rejoice in the streets, as they met the victorious army at the gate, and led them through the city. The defeated enemy would be paraded in chains, naked and disgraced, before the king and citizens of the victorious nation. They would be put to an open shame, helpless and humiliated. Everyone in the vanquished nation knew they had been defeated.

Jesus did this to Satan and his followers! Paul described it this way, *having disarmed principalities and powers, He made a public spectacle of them, triumphing over them in it (Colossians 2:15).* "Disarmed" means to strip off, disrobe, and to take away their weapons.

Four thousand years before, Satan had deceived Adam and Eve, and they had willfully surrendered their authority and dominion over this earth. Satan had become the conquering ruler, and humanity had been left stripped, naked and humiliated.

Now, Jesus had defeated Satan and all his demon forces, and Satan and his followers were left stripped, naked and humiliated. Satan had lost his dominion and authority over the human race and the earth.

Jesus had snatched the keys to Hades away from Satan. On the Isle of Patmos, Jesus proclaimed to John, *I am He who lives, and was dead, and behold, I am alive forevermore. Amen. And I have the keys of Hades and of Death (Revelation 1:18).* The keys, representing the authority, had been taken from Satan.

Satan and all of his demons, now defeated and humiliated, could no longer keep Jesus in the place of death. On the third day, the mighty power of God burst forth and Jesus rose victorious from the grave.

In a demonstration of His mighty power, Jesus had come forth from the grave. Now, with the keys in His hand, He ascended toward heaven.

Paul told the Ephesians of this great triumph of Jesus, ... *When He ascended on high, He led captivity captive, and gave gifts to men. (Now this, "He ascended"— what does it mean but that He also first descended into the lower parts of the earth? He who descended is also the One who ascended far above all the heavens, that He might fill all things) (Ephesians 4:8-10).*

When Jesus ascended, shouts of victory echoed throughout the corridors of heaven. The angels raised their voices together in an overwhelming crescendo of praise and joy.

David was given the words to describe this scene, *Lift up your heads, O you gates! And be lifted up, you everlasting doors! And the King of glory shall come in.*

Who is this King of glory? The Lord strong and mighty, The Lord mighty in battle.

Lift up your heads, O you gates! And lift them up, you everlasting doors! And the King of glory shall come in.

Who is this King of glory? The Lord of hosts, He is the King of glory (Psalms 24:7-10).

The King of Glory had returned to heaven. The Lord, strong and mighty, had returned to heaven victorious. When He approached the throne, His voice must have risen above the joyous shouts of the angels as He held His nail-scarred hands toward the Father.

I can picture the Father as He stood to His feet, and spread out His arms in welcome as love and joy radiated from His face.

"I have the keys! Father, I have the keys! Satan's defeated and I have the keys!" The emotion of that moment is beyond description. It's beyond the emotions that a human can feel. The Father, who three days earlier had turned His back on His Son because of the sins of the world that Jesus had taken upon Himself, was now lovingly embracing and accepting His only begotten Son back to Himself.

The Son of God took His own blood and sprinkled it over the mercy seat. The sacrifice of the Lamb of God had been made. The perfect justice of God was satisfied. Sin's penalty had been paid.

Redemption was complete.

Chapter Five

Authority Restored

Almost two thousand years have passed since that triumphant day when Jesus ascended to the Father.

However, when we look around the world today, we see millions of men, women and children who have never heard the name of Jesus. Millions of people who don't know that Jesus came to set them free.

On my frequent trips to India, I see thousands living in hopeless despair. They are worshiping gods they have fashioned with their own hands. Hunger, destitution, disease and death are evident from the Himalayan Mountains in the north to the tropical beaches and cities of Kerala State in the south.

One time in India, I saw the body of a young man hanging from a tree beside the road. He had committed suicide. The apathy was so great in that area that no one cared enough to take his body down.

In Central and South America, in Asia and Africa, all over the world, I have seen people living and dying in the same distress and terrible need.

Even in the wealthy cities of America, you can drive through sections of town and see people who are living in hunger, poverty and despair, existing, crowded together in tenements, and on the streets.

Corruption exists throughout our country. The streets of our cities are unsafe. Many of our schools are controlled by people who teach godless humanism. Satan worship and occult activity are becoming widespread. Immorality has become an accepted way of life.

Christian families are being destroyed. Young people are rebelling and their minds are being destroyed from using drugs and alcohol. Divorce is rampant.

Our hospitals are filled with men, women, and children who are struggling in a desperate fight for their lives. Even our advanced medical science has failed to stop the feared disease of cancer.

If Satan and his demonic forces were defeated nearly two thousand years ago, why are they able to continue their destruction today? Have the death of Jesus and the defeat of Satan become of no effect? What can we, as Christians, do to protect our marriages, our families, schools, communities, businesses, and finances against the attacks of the enemy?

When we discover the answers to these important questions, we will be encouraged and renewed in our determination to stop Satan's attempts to defeat us and our families.

After Satan and his demons were paraded before the spirit world in utter defeat, they remained on planet earth where they had been sent when they were cast out of heaven following their rebellion. Though still suffering from the effects of sin and the curse, this world was no longer under Satan's authority.

Satan, defeated and humiliated by Jesus, hated human beings even more. Because of God's love for these special creatures, Jesus had come to earth as a man and had defeated him.

At first, in a vicious attack against the new Christians, Satan tried persecution. From the book of Acts, we know this caused the believers to disperse and multiply. They traveled everywhere preaching the gospel, and as a result, thousands of people heard the message of freedom from the bondage of sin. Satan even lost his number one persecutor, Saul, who met the Lord on the road to Damascus.

"No," Satan must have thought, "My counterattack must be less obvious. I'll try deception again. It's always worked on human beings. It'll work now. In some way, I must keep them from knowing their position in Jesus Christ. They mustn't understand their regained authority. They mustn't find out about my defeat."

If humans could be deceived about their authority, Satan could use his fiery darts of guilt and condemnation. Men and women, in a state of confusion, would believe Satan's lie. They would believe that God was putting disease, and poverty on them to punish them.

"I'll be able to carry out my plans to destroy these creatures, and they'll blame it on God," Satan gloated. "If I can keep them from knowing their authority has been restored, they'll be helpless. I'll deceive them so completely they'll continue waiting in despair for God to do something to help them."

Satan concentrated his attention on creating a counterfeit religion. He made it as close as he could to

God's plan so people would believe it, but it was a religion without power and authority.

Soon, most of humanity was blinded by Satan's deception. Gradually, men and women stopped walking in the authority and power that Christ had regained for them. Without an understanding of this truth, they lost the vision of going into the world and preaching the good news of salvation and deliverance to every creature.

Satan extended his plans to use intimidation. Once men and women had lost the power they had in Jesus, Satan put fear into their hearts by demonstrations of his power. Christians were afraid to even talk about him, or in any way provoke his wrath. Men and women soon preferred to think of Satan as a small cartoon character with horns and a tail, running around in a red suit, carrying a pitchfork.

Deceived, they were again held in destitution, illness, and disease.

Satan's deception grew to the point that men and women even began to blame God for their condition and to cry out, "Why's God letting this happen to me?"

Satan has never forgotten, that at all costs, men and women must be kept from understanding the good news of redemption and total forgiveness through Jesus Christ!

However, in the midst of this hopelessness, the words of Jesus ring out, *And you shall know the truth, and the truth shall make you free (John 8:32).*

In these last days, God's revealing and restoring the truth of men and women's position of dominion and authority. The good news is that we are no longer bound to Satan's kingdom of darkness. We have been delivered! We are free! We are now in a new kingdom — the kingdom of God's Son, Jesus.

In Luke, we read that we had been captives of Satan, and that Jesus had come *to preach deliverance to the captives (Luke 4:18b).*

The apostle Paul, wrote to the Colossians, that God *has delivered us from the power of darkness and translated us into the kingdom of the Son of His Love (Colossians 1:13).* He continued, *in whom we have redemption through His blood, the forgiveness of sins. He is the image of the invisible God, the firstborn over all creation (Colossians 1:14,15).*

Jesus was the firstborn, and those who accept God's redemption and forgiveness are the ones born afterwards. Jesus explained this to Nicodemus when He said to him, *unless one is born again, he cannot see the kingdom of God (John 3:3b).* It's by this new birth that we are translated into the kingdom of His Son.

The moment we placed our faith in Jesus as Savior, the Holy Spirit took us and united us with the body of Christ. We became bone of His bone, and flesh of His flesh.

Jesus is the head of the body. He's in heaven, and in the spirit we are seated with Him in heavenly places. All that Christ has is ours, because we are in Him. We share His righteousness, His blessings and riches. Even while our position is with Him in heaven, we.are His body on earth.

In his first letter to the Corinthians, Paul wrote *For as the body is one and has many members, but all the members of that one body, being many, are one body, so also is Christ (1 Corinthians 12:12).* Paul describes us as His hands, His arms, His legs, and His feet.

It isn't a tragedy that Jesus only lived in His human body for thirty-three years. It isn't a disaster that His public ministry lasted only about three and a half years.

The truth revealed in these passages of Scripture is that Jesus' body is still alive on earth today. His body is the church that's made up of every believer in Jesus Christ. His ministry isn't over! It's going on today as His body is going into all the world preaching the good news to every creature.

As His body, we can now say as Jesus did at Nazareth, *The spirit of the Lord is upon Me, because He has anointed Me to preach the gospel to the poor. He has sent Me to heal the brokenhearted, to preach deliverance to the captives and recovering of sight to the blind, to set at liberty those who are oppressed (Luke 4:18).*

Much to the dismay of Satan, Jesus' body is no longer limited to being in one village at a time. Now, His body is in villages, cities and countries all over the world. He's preaching redemption to the poor, healing to the brokenhearted, and deliverance to the captives. His body is casting devils out of the oppressed, laying hands on the sick, and preaching liberty and victory to those who are bruised and discouraged.

We are His body! He is in us. When we arrive at a place of need, Jesus arrives at that place. When we preach the gospel, Jesus is speaking through us. When we cast out a devil, it's Jesus in us doing the work. When we lay our hands on the blind, the deaf and the lame, it's the arms and hands of Jesus that are still stretching forth to heal.

The devil thought the ministry of Jesus was over when he saw His body hanging on the cross. Instead, today he's faced with an even greater body. We are that body. We are the arms, hands and feet of Jesus. We are a body that can't be stopped, that's carrying the message of Jesus to the entire world.

In Ephesians, the apostle Paul recorded one of his prayers for the body of Christ. He prayed that they would really know and experience *the exceeding greatness of His power toward us who believe, according to the working of His mighty power which He worked in Christ when He raised Him from the dead and seated Him at His right hand in the heavenly places, far above all principality and power and might and dominion, and every name that is named, not only in this age but also in that which is to come.*

And He put all things under His feet, and gave Him to be head over all things to the church, which is His body, the fullness of Him who fills all in all (Ephesians 1:19-23).

In this passage, Paul said that the church, which is His body is the fullness of Him (Jesus) who fills all in all. We have become his "fullness." We might ask, if we, His church, are filling a void or an emptiness in the Son of God, what caused this emptiness? When did it occur?

Perhaps the answer to this question can be found by going back to the time Lucifer, "the anointed cherub that covers" was cast from heaven with his angels. Ezekiel described Lucifer's original function in heaven as one that required him to be right beside the throne of God, even as depicted by the angels who's wings covered the mercy seat above the ark of the covenant.

The mercy seat was a graphic, earthly picture of God's throne in heaven. The angels on each side of the mercy seat, who covered the throne with their wings, were to portray a function of "covering" that had taken place in heaven. This covering was obviously done by the angels of highest rank. They were chosen by God to be at His side.

It is interesting that even as there was a trinity in the Godhead, there appeared to be a trinity in the leadership of the angels. The Scriptures reveal that these leaders were Michael, Gabriel and Lucifer.

Each appeared to have a third of the angels under his leadership. When Lucifer rebelled and was cast out of heaven, John recorded that *His tail drew a third of the stars* (angels) *of heaven and threw them to the earth (Revelation 12:4a).*

John wrote that the one-third of the angels who followed Lucifer in his rebellion were "his" angels. *And war broke out in heaven: Michael and his angels fought against the dragon; and the dragon and his angels fought, but they did not prevail, nor was a place found for them in heaven any longer. So the great dragon was cast out, that serpent of old, called the Devil and Satan, who deceives the whole world; he was cast to the earth, and his angels were cast out with him (Revelation 12:7-9).*

John wrote that Michael had "his angels" and Lucifer had "his angels." Since Lucifer's angels were made up of one-third of the angels of heaven, we can assume that Michael's angels were another third, and that Gabriel must have had the other third under his command.

Each of the leading angels and the angels under their commands had different and distinctive functions to perform. Michael was the only one called the "archangel" so we can assume that he and the angels under him were to minister to the Father. They are revealed in Scripture as the warrior angels. They fought against "the dragon and his angels."

It was Michael that came to the aid of the angel who when dispatched to help Daniel, found himself engaged in a twenty-one day battle with the "prince of Persia." It was Michael who "contended with the devil" in a dispute over the body of Moses.

Gabriel always appeared as the messenger angel. He was sent from the presence of God to announce the birth of both John the Baptist and Jesus. Gabriel revealed the work of the Holy Spirit when he told Mary, *The Holy Spirit will come upon you, and the power of the Highest will overshadow you; therefore, also, that Holy One who is to be born will be called the Son of God (Luke 1:35)*. It appears therefore that Gabriel and his angels are the angels who minister to the Holy Spirit.

Could it be that Lucifer was the one whose primary function was to minister to the Son of God? He provided a "covering" of praise and worship as He led his angels in ministering day and night before the throne in beautiful music and songs of adoration.

When there was rebellion, and Lucifer and his angels were cast out of heaven, how was this void filled? Did the Father ask Michael and Gabriel to reassign some of their angels to fill this void in ministering to the Son in praise and worship before the throne?

Could it be that when God created men and women in His image, to be worshipers of Him, to be seated with Him in heavenly places, to be at His side as His "fullness" and to rule and reign with Him through out eternity, they were created to fill the void left by Lucifer and his angels?

Men and women, created in God's image, can only be complete and fulfilled when the Creator once again breathes His life into them at the moment of salvation. He fills the emptiness in their lives with Himself. Now, they are to fulfill Him by giving themselves to Him in praise and worship.

When we praise and worship God, we are not only fulfilling the former function of Lucifer and his angels, we are demonstrating the fact that they are defeated and have no place in heaven. When we raise our hands to the Son of God, we are fulfilling Him with our praise and worship. When we dance before Him, it is as though our feet are bruising the head of the devil. We are trampling him and all of his demons under our feet. Demons start to flee when we begin to praise and worship God. The enemy is defeated when we begin to minister to the Lord in praise and worship.

Praise is a mighty weapon God has given us which releases His power to defeat the enemy.

King Jehoshaphat was faced with a seemingly impossible military situation when the armies of many nations had assembled in battle against the armies of Judah. *And when he had consulted with the people, he appointed those who should sing to the Lord, and who should praise the beauty of holiness, as they went out before the army and were saying: "Praise the LORD, His mercy endures forever." Now when they began to sing and to praise, the Lord set ambushes against the people of Ammon, Moab, and Mount Seir, who had come against Judah; and they were defeated (2 Chronicles 20:21,22).*

Today, if we are to fulfill our God ordained function and creative purpose, we too will become worshipers of God. As we do, we will be living in dominion and putting to flight "the armies of the aliens." Paul wrote that Jesus, the head of the body, is seated in heaven, far above Satan's kingdom. He went on to explain that the church, His body, is still on this earth. Christ is the head! He's in heaven. We are His body. We are His feet. All things are now under our feet! All principalities, powers, might, dominion, all of Satan's forces are now under our feet!

In Genesis, God has recorded the prophecy of the bruising of the head of Satan under the feet of Jesus. *And I will put enmity between you and the woman, and between your seed and her Seed; He shall bruise your head, and you shall bruise His heel (Genesis 3:15).* We are the feet of Jesus on this earth.

The writer of the book of Hebrews asked, *What is man that You are mindful of him, or the son of man that You take care of him (Hebrews 2:6b)?*

You made him a little lower than the angels; (literally "Elohim," or God), *You crowned him with glory and honor, and set him over the works of Your hands.*

You have put all things in subjection under his feet. For in that He put all in subjection under him, He left nothing that is not put under him (Hebrews 2:7,8a).

In the beginning, God created man and woman and put all things on this earth in subjection to them. They were to rule over this earth and everything in it. However, they lost this dominion and for four thousand years they lived under the dominion of the ruler of the darkness, a kingdom under the control of Satan.

The writer of the book of Hebrews goes on to say, *But now we do not yet see all things put under him. But we see Jesus, who was made a little lower than the angels, for the suffering of death crowned with glory and honor, that He, by the grace of God, might taste death for everyone.*

Inasmuch then as the children have partaken of flesh and blood, He Himself likewise shared in the same, that through death He might destroy him who had the power of death, that is, the devil, and release those who through fear of death were all their lifetime subject to bondage (Hebrews 2:8b,9,14,15).

Jesus, through His death, destroyed the devil! He brought to nought the devil and made him of no effect. Jesus made the devil a big "zero." His authority and dominion were destroyed!

Paul told the believers in Rome, *And the God of peace will crush Satan under your feet shortly (Romans 16:20a)*. Now, as the body and feet of Jesus, we are to demonstrate Satan's defeat. We are to bruise his head under our feet. We are not to live under Satan's dominion. We are not in his kingdom of darkness where he held men for thousands of years as poor, broken-hearted captives, bruised by demonic powers.

The first seventy followers that Jesus sent out to minister had just returned to Him, filled with joy. They said, *"Lord, even the demons are subject to us in Your name."*

Jesus replied, *"I saw Satan fall like lightning from heaven.*

"Behold, I give you the authority to trample on serpents and scorpions, and over all the power of the enemy, and nothing shall by any means hurt you (Luke 10:17b,18,19)."

Jesus took this opportunity to explain to them that He had given them power, or authority to tread on that old serpent, the devil, and all his demon powers. As they were delighting over their new authority over the underlings, the demons, Jesus told them that they need no longer fear the ruler, Satan, himself! Jesus had come to set them free and to restore their authority. Satan would be under their feet as long as they continued to exercise that authority.

It thrilled Jesus that this important truth had been revealed to His disciples, and we are allowed to share His prayer of rejoicing offered to the Father at this very moment. *In that hour Jesus rejoiced in Spirit and said, "I praise You, Father, Lord of heaven and earth, that You have hidden these things from the wise and prudent and revealed them to babes (Luke 10:21a)."*

Jesus rejoiced that the Father had revealed this truth to His followers, babes in the spirit world. They had received revelation knowledge. They were beginning to walk in their new authority in the spirit realm!

As the Father, by His Holy Spirit, is now revealing the truth of our authority to us, I believe that Jesus is rejoicing again. He died to set us free! He died to regain for us authority over Satan!

We have been delivered from the power of darkness and placed into the kingdom of God. We are seated with Christ in heavenly places. We are in Him. We share His kingship. We are now reigning and ruling with Him. We share His authority and dominion.

Many Christians are rejoicing in this revelation knowledge. Many are awakening to this great truth. At last, they know who they are in Christ Jesus. They know they no longer need to live in defeat. Instead, they are putting Satan and his demons under their feet. They are demonstrating the fact that he's a defeated foe. Confidently and boldly, they are rising from poverty, disease, and despair. With heads held high, they are beginning to walk in their new-found authority and dominion.

Chapter Six

Look Out Satan,
Here Comes the Church!

Sandy was a supervisor in a large food processing plant in California. She had been a Sunday school teacher for many years in a denominational church in her home town, but she knew little about a living Jesus who wanted to be part of her life on a daily basis.

One evening she attended a meeting where she heard that Jesus was more than an historical figure and she asked Him to take over her life as her Savior. Following that decision, Sandy began looking for a Bible study where she could find Christian fellowship and grow in her new-found faith.

She heard about a Tuesday night fellowship that met at our home, and the next week she came to the meeting. She experienced the presence of God in a new and greater dimension as we sang songs of praise and worship to the Lord. At times, the atmosphere of the room was super-charged with the presence and power of Jesus. Sandy was amazed when the Lord confirmed His Word and demonstrated His presence by several healings.

The following week, she brought some of her friends to the meeting. One accepted Jesus as her Savior, and another received a miraculous back healing. The news began to spread, and week after week, others from that company would come to our home.

The excitement and expectancy grew as many met Jesus as their Savior, Lord and Healer.

Soon, Sandy and the others began to pray for fellow-workers in the plant. Miracles began to happen while people worked on the assembly lines and in the offices. Many found Jesus as their Savior during the lunch periods and coffee breaks. An exciting revival swept through the company and it seemed everyone was talking about Jesus. God confirmed His Word with signs and miracles on a daily basis.

There had been a witch's coven operating for many years in this plant. The head witch, Evelyn, was an employee also. Many people, curious about the supernatural, had been deceived and had become involved in the occult through the teachings of this witch. She said there were good witches and bad witches, and of course, she was a good witch.

Christians had fallen prey to sickness, disease, and accidents because of this witch's curses and incantations. If someone, Christian or non-Christian, was in disfavor or stood in the way of the promotion of one of those in the coven, they would suddenly find themselves suffering tragedy in their lives. The evil power of this coven of witches was evident throughout the organization.

The Christians they had encountered before seemed weak and helpless and usually fell prey to their witchcraft. But now, a new power was being felt in the plant. Many people were coming to Jesus and being healed. The witches had never before encountered Christians with power and authority. They knew the devil had power, but they had never experienced the power of God.

Evelyn soon discovered that the source of this power seemed to center around the Tuesday night meetings at our home. She decided something must be done to stop them. The coven of witches changed their meeting to Tuesday night so they could bring a curse upon us and the fellowship.

We didn't know the witches were now meeting on the same evening. We continued praying for the salvation of many of them by name and were actively binding their efforts to disrupt the lives of the Christians at the plant.

One Tuesday evening, we were having a wonderful time worshiping and praising the Lord. Our attention was focused on Him and His goodness and blessings. Suddenly, a dark cloud came billowing toward the room. It was a tremendous wave of evil. In the spirit, several of us saw one black wave after another coming against our group. Several gasped at the sight and feeling of this horrible mass. A feeling of fear, even panic, began to fill the room as everyone stopped singing and sat in stunned silence.

I sprang to my feet, pointed my finger at that dark cloud, and exclaimed, "No! Satan, I bind you in the name of Jesus! You spirit of fear, leave this house right now! You will not disrupt this meeting. I take dominion over you. I break this curse and command you to leave in the name of Jesus!"

The moment I stood and said, "No!" the waves stopped. As I continued taking authority and dominion over them, the waves of evil started backing from the room as rapidly as they had come. They were piling up, one on top of another in their haste.

Joyce had jumped to her feet with me and when I stopped speaking, she began to speak in the same authority. She spoke exactly what the Holy Spirit was speaking to her. "I command you, in the name of Jesus, go back and attach yourself to the ones that sent you!" Immediately, the waves of terror, moved swiftly in the opposite direction. The fear was gone and our group began to praise the Lord for the victory.

It was then someone told us about the witches meeting on that night, and we realized what had happened. We had seen a manifestation of the battle that was taking place in the spirit world. We had seen a demonstration of the authority that we have as Christians over the forces of Satan.

The believers at that plant went back with an even bolder witness of the power of Jesus Christ to change lives and many others met Jesus as their Savior. Several weeks later, Sandy was working next to the head witch at the plant. She casually asked, "Evelyn, are you folks still meeting Tuesday nights?"

Evelyn turned away and, in obvious frustration answered, "No ... Well, ah ... Something ... The last time we met, something backfired! We don't meet any more."

That is the authority we have in the name of Jesus! Whatever happened at the witch's meeting when that cloud of evil was sent back had scared them so badly that it had broken up the witch's coven.

What did happen in the spirit world that night? When I exclaimed, "Satan, I bind you," why did the demon forces have to obey me? How could I break the powerful curse that had been sent against us by simply speaking words? What was the source of this authority?

Matthew related a conversation that he and the other disciples had with Jesus. Jesus asked His disciples, *"Who do men say that I, the Son of man, am?"*

So they said, "Some say John the Baptist, some Elijah, and others Jeremiah or one of the prophets (Matthew 16:13b,14)."

Today, many religious leaders are saying that "Jesus was a good teacher," or that "He was a great religious leader." Many fail to realize who Jesus really is and what He has done for them through His death and resurrection. They do not understand that He came to destroy the works of the devil. They do not know the great victory that He accomplished when He descended into the dark region of Satan's kingdom and spoiled principalities and powers.

Others fail to realize that He is the Christ of the resurrection; the one whom Satan and all his forces could not keep in the grave.

First, Jesus asked, *Who do men say that I, the Son of man, am?* Then, He brought His question beyond the empty answers of a powerless religion. He made His question personal when He went on to ask, *But who do you say that I am?*

It is the answer to that question that delivers us from the power of darkness into the kingdom of God. It is the answer to that question that sets us free from Satan's dominion. When we begin to realize who Jesus is, and then, to understand all that He is, we now are, we can be set free! We are one in Him. We are bone of His bone, and flesh of His flesh. We are His body. Jesus is alive on earth today in us.

And Simon Peter answered and said, "You are the Christ, the Son of the living God (Matthew 16:16)."

Peter understood. The Son of the living God had been revealed to him. Peter knew he was talking to a living God! God was not dead then, and He is still alive today. In His resurrection, He conquered sin, Hades, death, Satan and his demonic forces.

As I have traveled in nations around the world, and have seen the gods of many religions, I have realized that all these gods have had one thing in common. They are all non-existent or dead. Our God is alive.

Jesus answered and said to him, "Blessed are you, Simon Bar-Jonah, for flesh and blood has not revealed this to you, but My Father who is in heaven (Matthew 16:17)."

Just as the Father desired to reveal His Son, Jesus, in that day, He desires to reveal Him to the world today.

Jesus went on to say, *And I also say to you that you are Peter, and on this rock I will build My church (Matthew 16:18a).* Peter's name meant "a small rock," but Jesus spoke of "the rock" on which His church was to be built. That rock was the revelation of Christ, the Son of the living God.

What was this new thing that Jesus was talking about? What was a church? The spiritual life in that day centered around the local synagogue and the temple in Jerusalem. But now, Jesus had mentioned something new, something that He was going to build. How was He going to build it? What was its purpose?

God revealed, in the New Testament, that the church was made up of every man, woman and child who received the message of salvation through Jesus Christ. It was His body on this earth. Paul wrote to the Ephesians that God *gave Him to be head over all things to the church, which is His body, the fullness of Him who fills all in all (Ephesians 1:22b,23)*.

Jesus went on to describe this powerful church when He said, *and the gates of Hades shall not prevail against it (Matthew 16:18b)*.

The gates of Hades refer to the governments of Satan. During the period of the Old Testament, much of the legal business and governing was done at the gates. An example of this is when Daniel sat in the gate of King Nebuchadnezzar as the *ruler over the whole province of Babylon (Daniel 2:48,49)*.

Jesus said that He would build His body on earth, so strong, so full of authority, dominion and power that the gates of hell, the council and government of Satan, could not stop it.

For years, when I sang the words of a song, "Hold the fort for I am coming," I falsely pictured the believers anxiously cowering behind the gates. In my mental picture, Satan and his forces were attacking the body of Christ from the outside much like the Indians would attack the frontier forts in the early days of the United States.

I knew that the world situation was getting worse and worse. It seemed that there were only a few real Christians left. It seemed we were losing the battle and the devil was winning. I felt overwhelmed with the evil forces that were taking over the world. I thought that if the faithful few could hold out a little longer, just before we were totally defeated, just before Satan made his final attack on our little fort, Jesus would return for His church and rescue us.

However, Jesus declared to His disciples that He would build a church that the gates of Hades could not prevail against. One day I realized that we are not to cower in anxious fear. We are not on the defense! We are on the offense! We are to be the ones doing the attacking!

Satan and his demonic forces should be cowering behind the gates! Gates do not attack us. We attack them. The very gates of hell, the government of Satan, cannot hold up against the attack of God's army.

The church is alive and well. The church has been given authority over all the power of the enemy. Today, an army of believers, called by the name of Jesus, is storming the gates of the enemy. This army is forcefully advancing the kingdom of God throughout the world. This army of God is moving and Satan and his forces are on the run.

We are at no disadvantage when dealing with Satan. He is a defeated foe! It is his fort that is under attack and Jesus said that his gates could not prevail against us.

When God created man in a body that looked just like His, and breathed into him His own breath of life, the first thing that He said about man was, *let them have dominion.* This was to be man's primary responsibility on this earth.

When Jesus mentioned His new body, the very first thing He said about the church was, *And the gates of Hades shall not prevail against it (Matthew 16:18).* The first responsibility Jesus gave the church was to storm the gates of Hades, as they move in their newly restored authority and dominion.

When Jesus talked to Peter and the other disciples about this new church, He said, *And I will give you the keys of the kingdom of heaven, and whatever you bind on earth will be bound in heaven, and whatever you loose on earth will be loosed in heaven (Matthew 16:19).*

Satan held the keys to the kingdoms of the world when he tempted Jesus in the wilderness. He took Jesus *up on an exceedingly high mountain, and showed Him all the kingdoms of the world and their glory. And he said to Him, "All these things I will give You if You will fall down and worship me (Matthew 4:8b,9)."*

Satan had dangled those keys in front of Jesus. He knew that Jesus had come to take those keys back and he had used them in his attempt to deceive Jesus.

Jesus knew the Father's plan for the restoration of those keys to humanity had to be won by a man living perfectly on this earth and then giving up His life willingly as a sacrifice for sin.

These were the keys that Jesus stripped from Satan's grasp at the very gates of hell. These were the keys that Jesus had in His hands when He ascended to the Father and marched triumphantly up to the throne of God.

In the book of Revelation, we see Jesus in that moment of triumph when He joyfully declared to the Hosts of Heaven, *I am He who lives, and was dead, and behold, I am alive forevermore. Amen. And I have the keys of Hades and of Death (Revelation 1:18).*

The keys represent the authority and dominion that God gave Adam when He placed him on this earth. They represent the authority Adam surrendered to Satan. Satan, with the keys of authority in his hands, had become the god of this world, the ruler of the darkness of this earth. Now, Satan has been stripped of his authority, disarmed of his power, and put to an open shame in his defeat.

Jesus announced to His disciples that He would give these keys back to His body on this earth. When He defeated Satan, He took the keys from him and gave them back to humanity. Now, once again, redeemed men and women were truly as God created them to be. They again had dominion over the kingdoms of this world.

Today, Satan does not have the keys! Jesus does not have the keys! We, the church of Jesus Christ, have the keys, and with these keys of authority and dominion in our hands, the gates of hell should not prevail against us.

For years I cried out, "Lord, why are you letting Satan do this to me? Why are you letting Satan destroy my health, my finances, my family? Why are you letting Satan destroy our churches, our schools, our cities, our nation? Lord, why don't you help me? Why don't you stop this awful attack of the devil?"

If I had stopped crying long enough and had listened to what God was saying, I would have heard Him say, "Nothing! I'm not going to do anything about the work of the devil! Jesus has already done it! His work was complete almost two thousand years ago.

"It cost me the death of my Son on the cross to redeem you and restore your authority. I have given you the keys of authority over the power of the enemy. It is up to you to use those keys to demonstrate Satan's defeat."

What can Satan do to Christians today? What can he do to our health, families, finances, churches, schools, cities and even our nation? Only what we let him do!

We only lose today because we are ignorant of these facts, or because we have been taken in by Satan's deception. Satan has deceived us for years into thinking he has more power than we do. He's a liar, a robber, and the master of deception.

Today, there is arising an army of men and women who have discovered who they are in Jesus. They have discovered the good news of their restored authority and dominion. They have determined in their hearts that Satan is no longer going to bring his destruction into their lives. They have taken these wonderful keys into their hands and are demonstrating to the world that Satan is defeated. They are more than conquerors through Jesus Christ.

Jesus said that with these keys of authority, whatever is bound on earth, shall be bound in heaven.

When we stood against that cloud of evil in our living room on that Tuesday evening, we moved in authority over the devil. That's why Satan had to obey us. That's why the curse was broken. That's why the dark cloud of fear immediately left the room. That's why a coven of witches and Satan worshipers disbanded. We had discovered our authority. We had demonstrated the fact that Satan was a defeated foe!

Jesus said, *But if I cast out demons by the Spirit of God, surely the kingdom of God has come upon you. Or else how can one enter a strong man's house and plunder his goods, unless he first binds the strong man? And then he will plunder his house* (Matthew 12:28,29).

The word that Jesus used in Matthew when He said to bind the strong man means: to fasten, or tie, as with chains, like an animal is chained to a stake to keep him restrained. Satan can only go so far, and no farther. Satan can be bound. He can be made inoperative and restrained from his work. His power can be cut off.

When we bind the strong man, we are able to spoil his house. We are able to exercise dominion and authority by casting out the principalities, powers, rulers of the darkness of this world, and spiritual wickedness in high places. We are able to be like the heroes of faith described in the book of Hebrews *who through faith subdued kingdoms, worked righteousness, obtained promises, stopped the mouths of lions, quenched the violence of fire, escaped the edge of the sword, out of weakness were made strong, became valiant in battle, turned to flight the armies of the aliens* (Hebrews 11:33,34).

When we look at the kingdoms of the world today, we see the communist countries that had been holding millions of people in bondage, now open to the gospel. We see countries where Islam has been in control for centuries and yet there is a hunger in the hearts of the people to know Jesus. We see China where communism still holds millions in bondage and yet the church is multiplying rapidly.

The Word of God says that Jesus is going to build His church and the gates of Hades will not prevail against it.

Believers are forming a spiritual army today that knows their *struggle is not against flesh and blood, but against the rulers, against the authorities, against the powers of this dark world and against the spiritual forces of evil in the heavenly realm (Ephesians 6:12).* They have discovered their *weapons are not carnal, but mighty through God, to the pulling down of strongholds (2 Corinthians 10:4).*

These awakened believers are beginning to use their spiritual authority. They are binding the enemy and are storming the gates of hell. They are not afraid of the power of Satan.

When China fell to communism, missionaries were driven from the country. Pastors were killed. Bibles and other Christian books were burned. Thousands of Christians were imprisoned, tortured, and even killed for their faith. Children were taken from their parents and were raised and indoctrinated by a godless government. The people of China were held in bondage to godless materialism.

When this persecution started, an estimated one hundred thousand believers were spread throughout the country.

Surely, the gospel of Jesus Christ had been stopped. The flame of the gospel must have flickered and gone out by this time. Satan must have won the battle to stamp out the name of Jesus while he had such complete control of China.

But when the bamboo curtain parted to allow trade with the Western world, reports began to come from Chinese believers. From these reports, we have learned the number of Christians in China has grown from about one hundred thousand before the communist persecution to close to fifty million today.

Through this opening in the curtain, we know the underground church is meeting in homes throughout the land. Thousands of Bibles are pouring across China and revival is sweeping the nation. There are reports of miraculous healings and even stories of the dead who have been brought back to life.

The gates of hell have not been able to prevail against the body of Christ in China even with the total control that has been exercised by the communist government.

In May of 1988, Joyce and I were conducting meetings in Helsinki, Finland, a short distance from the Russian border. President Reagan and the Secretary of State were in Helsinki at the same time. They were leaving the next day to go to Moscow for a summit meeting that resulted in a major change in East-West relations.

As we began the meeting that night, Joyce and I felt impressed to go into spiritual warfare with the forces of darkness that had held the people of the Soviet Union captive for so many years. We felt an urgency in our spirits to release the power of God into the coming summit meeting. We were particularly burdened for the Russian Jews who were being denied permission to leave Russia and for the Christians to be given freedom to worship.

I briefly taught the believers and Christian leaders who had gathered for the meeting about our overcoming authority in the name of Jesus. I reminded them that the gates of hell cannot prevail against the church which has a revelation of its restored authority and dominion.

I asked the crowd to stand and point their hands toward Russia and then I felt impressed to give the microphone to Joyce. She began to speak with boldness and great authority to the forces of darkness inside the communist world. As the Holy Spirit led, she commanded the communist leaders to allow the Jewish people to leave that land. She commanded them to allow the Christians to worship in freedom.

We were, geographically and spiritually, at the gates of the enemy as we stood in Helsinki that night. The warfare was intense. We knew in the spirit that we were "putting to flight the armies of the aliens." In just a few minutes, we knew the breakthrough had come. Later, Joyce shared with me that as she spoke in the power of the Holy Spirit, she had seen something like "lightening bolts" exploding all over the Soviet Union.

Certainly, we were not the only ones who were led by the Holy Spirit to go into warfare at that time. People all over the world must have been led to pray for that historic summit meeting. Our group had joined in faith with hundreds or perhaps thousands of believers who knew their authority in the name of Jesus and had gone into victorious spiritual warfare.

During the summit meeting, top priority was given to the areas for which we had prayed. As a result, a major exodus of Soviet Jews began as they were now allowed to leave Russia. Many began making their way to Israel in fulfillment of Biblical prophecy.

The walls of communism began to crumble. To the amazement of the world, the Berlin wall was torn down. The stronghold of the communist party over the Soviet Union crumbled almost overnight. An unprecedented open door to preach the gospel swung open. The gospel could be preached openly, even on national television, and hundreds of thousands of precious people received Jesus as their Savior.

One by one, nations that had been held captive by the communists for many years, declared their independence and once again their doors were wide open to the gospel of Jesus Christ.

Almost to the shock of the Christian world, we had seen a mighty demonstration of the fact that "the gates of Hades shall not prevail" against a church which has discovered their mighty overcoming dominion in the name of Jesus.

Satan has been able to lock up and imprison millions of people on this earth because believers have let him do it. The body of Christ has been deceived by Satan into thinking they are a helpless minority. The church has lost its power. It has forgotten, or neglected to walk in its authority.

But our generation of believers is awakening to an awareness of our restored dominion. Once again, the parting words of Jesus are ringing in our spirits. He said, *Go into all the world and preach the gospel to every creature (Mark 16:15b).*

No curtain, wall, or gate can stop believers who know who they are in Christ Jesus. The gospel can, and must, be taken to every creature on earth today. In the history of the church, this is the most exciting time to be alive. For this is the generation that will fulfill the great commission and go to all the world taking the gospel to every creature.

There are more people alive on the face of the earth today than have lived and died throughout all the ages of the world's history. With the tools of modern communication and transportation, armed with the authority and commission of Jesus Christ, we can and will, be a part of the believers who will reach the world with the gospel.

Christians, discovering for the first time their authority and dominion in the spirit realm, are throwing off the shackles of sickness, disease and poverty. For years their thoughts have been so involved with their own problems and limitations that they have lost the vision of reaching the world for Jesus.

The church has been like a sleeping giant, but it is awakening. In its hands are the keys to the kingdoms of the world. The church is using these keys of authority to open the prison doors of the captives. The gates of hell will not prevail!

Chapter Seven

There's Power in the Blood

It was a cold winter New Year's Eve when the click of the switchblade knife could be heard above the crackling of the fire in the fireplace. "I'm going to kill you," growled a demonic voice from deep within Bill. His penetrating blue eyes were fixed on me like those of a jungle cat ready to attack.

Bill had been a drummer with a famous acid-rock band in Southern California before he and his mother had received Jesus Christ as their Savior and started attending a local church. Bill had resigned from the rock band when he accepted Christ.

Demon voices had talked to Bill, night and day, for as long as he could remember. For years, he and his mother had seen tables moving and objects floating in various rooms of their home. Even after Bill had accepted Jesus into his life, he continued to hear the evil voices. Sometimes, they were talking to him. Other times, they were talking among themselves about him. The demonic manifestations around his home continued.

Bill was a brilliant young man. In addition to his musical abilities, he was gifted in mechanical design. But the demons were continually lying to him. They told him his creative and musical abilities came through them.

Bill's mother had gone to their pastor for help, but he believed Christians were not bothered by demons. Because of this belief, he refused to pray with them about the problems they were having. She called several other Christian leaders, but no one offered any help. As Bill continued to grow worse, so did her fear and torment

In his early years in grade school, Bill had been in a vicious fight with a classmate, and he had won. This young, "defeated classmate" grew up to become the leader of the dreaded Chicano gang that controlled Bill's neighborhood. Consequently, Bill had become the enemy of the entire gang, and with his light blond hair, blue eyes, and fair skin, he could be easily spotted.

One day when he was riding home from school on his bicycle, some gang members deliberately ran into him with their car and knocked him down. The attacks grew worse. Another day when a van passed Bill, a shotgun was pointed out of the window, and the blast hit Bill in the knee. The front wall of his house was pitted with bullet holes.

Bill had designed and built a special, short gun that he carried in his back pack. It was designed in such a way, that he could pull it from the pack, aim and shoot it with one hand, as he continued to ride his bicycle.

He lived in daily fear for his life. The gang was trying to kill him. The demons tormented him and his family. It seemed there was no hope — no way out of his desperate situation.

Bill attended a nearby Christian high school and was a classmate and friend of our son, John. He was in and out of our home regularly for several years. We thought we knew him, but we did not know any of these things were happening in his life. Perhaps he was afraid we would turn him away, as his pastor and other Christians had done, if he told us. He never mentioned the personal fear, torment, or the despair he was feeling.

Then a few days before New Year's Eve, Bill awakened and found a death note on his pillow. He was a "marked man." The gang had decided to kill him at midnight on New Year's Eve. (Killings were not unusual in this neighborhood on the east side of Los Angeles.)

When he found the marked card on his pillow saying he was going to die, the demons within him agreed. He was going to die. They, and Bill, decided he would take his gun and start stalking the gang on New Year's Eve. He was going to kill them, one by one, until one of them killed him. His plan was to kill as many of them as he could before he died at midnight.

Our family had been vacationing at our mountain home since before Christmas. Just before New Year's, I was to make a trip back to Los Angeles for a business meeting. Immediately after the meeting, I would return to the mountains for the rest of our vacation.

John did not know Bill's immediate situation, but he felt impressed by God to make the trip to Los Angeles with me with the express purpose of bringing Bill back to the mountains.

Satan had made his plans, but God had a counter plan already in motion! John felt such an urgency when he was talking to Bill that he would not take "no" for an answer. He insisted until he finally convinced Bill to come and spend the rest of the holidays with us. Unknown to us, these were the very days the gang and the demons had planned for Bill to die.

During the two-hour drive back to the mountains, I began to share with Bill the many miracles we had seen God perform. In return, he began to tell me about a few of the attacks on his life.

That evening, as we were sitting in our family room, the gift of the discerning of spirits began to operate. I said, "Bill, God has revealed some things to me about your life and the trouble you are in."

When he indicated a desire for me to continue, I spoke by revelation. I told him of the tormenting demons, how they had been lying to him, and were even trying to kill him. Then I shared with him the good news that Jesus wanted to set him free.

Immediately, his eyes narrowed, and his voice changed. An unbelievably evil voice began to come from him. The Bill we knew almost disappeared as his facial expressions changed and even his mannerisms.

We began to obey the Lord's instructions to *Resist the devil and he will flee from you (James 4:7b)*. We bound Satan, and then, when God revealed them to us, we began to command the demon spirits to leave.

The demon spirits said through Bill's changed voice, "We've got to get Bill out of this house."

"You have to leave, but Bill's going to stay!" I firmly replied.

Bill started for the front door. John jumped in front of him to prevent him from going outside. He knew Bill's life would be endangered if he ran out into the freezing night and became lost in the national forest behind our home. Bill sat down and we continued to demand that the demons leave.

Suddenly, Bill thrust his hand into the pocket of his blue jeans and pulled out a switchblade knife. He glared at me, his eyes flashing with hate, as the five inch blade of that knife flashed into view. "I'm going to kill you!" he exclaimed, as he jumped up and started across the room toward me.

I was sitting in a captain's chair, leaning back in a relaxed position, with only two legs of the chair on the floor. My hands were clasped behind my neck. In the natural, I was completely unprotected, but I felt no fear. Without changing my position to one of defense, I replied in total confidence, "You can't touch me! I'm covered with the blood of Jesus!"

By this time, Bill was halfway across the room, his knife coming straight toward my chest. Suddenly, he stopped and began to shrink back as he closed the knife. He grimaced as he hesitantly and with some difficulty said, "I know it. I know it! You are covered with that icky stuff."

Without pausing, he exclaimed, "It's all over you. It's all over her." He was looking at Joyce. "It's all over him." He was staring at John. "That icky stuff is all over the walls, the fireplace, everywhere! It's even all over your dog." By that time, he was almost snarling in disgust.

We knew what the demon meant, but would not say. Everything in our home was covered with the wonderful, precious blood of Jesus! Before we had started to minister to Bill, we had acknowledged, in faith, that the blood of Jesus covered us, our whole family and all of our property. Now, we knew we had discovered the area of greatest weakness in this enemy.

We repeated those powerful words over and over: "The blood of Jesus, the blood of Jesus." We reminded the demon spirits that it was the shed blood of Jesus on the cross that had redeemed Bill from their power.

We reminded them that Satan had been defeated almost two thousand years ago. We reminded them that every demon had been personally defeated by the shed blood of Jesus and that His blood had never lost its power!

We continued to take authority over the demon spirits and command them to leave. Some demons would argue and say they didn't have to leave, but we confidently told them to come out in the name of Jesus.

A couple of hours had passed since we had begun ministering to Bill. All that remained of the fire in the fireplace was the occasional crackling of a glowing ember. As we continued, we wondered why it was taking so much time. However, we never questioned the fact that according to God's Word, he would be set completely free.

The Lord was giving us, through the spiritual gift of the word of knowledge, the exact name of many ruling demon spirits that had been tormenting Bill. One by one, we commanded them to leave.

Just as we felt a release in our spirits, Bill began to turn around and around on the tall stool where he was then seated. As he turned, the words came out, "I'm leaving. I'm leaving. I'm leaving." After three turns, a different Bill looked at us, and a beautiful smile of release spread across his face. I glanced at my watch. It was midnight, a New Year had begun. This was the exact time the demons had told Bill he would die.

Bill blinked his eyes, as if awakening from sleep. "Mr. Gill," he asked, "What's happening?" I looked into his clear eyes and exclaimed, "Bill, you have been set free by the blood of Jesus!" He suddenly realized the fear and torment were gone. He was not going to die! He no longer heard the voices. He felt more alive and peaceful than he could ever remember feeling in his life.

He slept soundly the rest of the night and he awakened the next morning in total peace. The whole world looked beautiful to him. He felt the excitement of new hope and meaning for his life. Bill had been set free through the power of the blood of Christ and by the authority that is available to every believer.

Joyce and I had an even greater appreciation for the protection of the blood of Jesus over our lives, our family, and our property. Certainly, Satan had been overcome by the blood of the Lamb.

When we look into God's Word we read, *And they overcame him* (Satan) *by the blood of the Lamb and by the word of their testimony (Revelation 12:11a).*

Why is the blood of Jesus called the blood of the Lamb? Why does the blood that flowed through the veins of Jesus have such a powerful effect on Satan and demon spirits today?

When John the Baptist saw Jesus approaching the Jordan River, he exclaimed, *Behold! The Lamb of God who takes away the sin of the world (John 1:29b)*! John was speaking by the inspiration of the Holy Spirit, who knew that the Messiah would be the final sacrifice. He knew Jesus was the Son of God, our sacrifice.

Jesus was the fulfillment of the sacrifices that had been offered for thousands of years according to the Old Testament law. At the temple in Jerusalem, as God had directed, the priests sacrificed innocent lambs, without spot or blemish, to atone for the sins of the people. Once a year, the high priest would carry the blood of a sacrificial lamb within the veil of the temple, into the Holy of Holies. This was the earthly dwelling place of God. It was the earthly counterpart to the throne room of heaven. The priest would sprinkle the blood over the mercy seat.

In the book of Hebrews, we are given a wonderful picture of the Old Testament sacrifices and their fulfillment, once and for all, by the sacrifice of Jesus Christ on the cross.

But into the second part (Holy of Holies) *the high priest went alone once a year, not without blood, which he offered for himself and for the people's sins committed in ignorance;*

But Christ came as High Priest of the good things to come, with the greater and more perfect tabernacle not made with hands, that is, not of this creation.

Not with the blood of goats and calves, but with His own blood He entered the Most Holy Place once for all, having obtained eternal redemption.

... how much more shall the blood of Christ, who through the eternal Spirit offered Himself without spot to God, purge your conscience from dead works to serve the living God?

... saying, "This is the blood of the covenant which God has commanded you."

... he sprinkled with blood both the tabernacle and all the vessels of the ministry.

And according to the law almost all things are purged with blood, and without shedding of blood there is no remission.

...but now, once at the end of the ages, He has appeared to put away sin by the sacrifice of Himself (Hebrews 9:7,11-26).

The tabernacle and the temple, the work and ministry of the priest, the articles of furniture, and the sacrifices were types, examples, visual pictures, of the Person and work of our true High Priest, Jesus Christ. He is not only our High Priest, but He became our sacrificial Lamb and shed His own blood for the remission of our sins.

After Jesus' death on the cross and His descent into the dark regions of Satan's kingdom, He not only defeated Satan and all of his demonic followers, but

He ascended far above them, into the very throne room of God, where He deposited His own blood, and by it, purchased our redemption.

Through sin, Satan had been successful in separating men and women from God. The human race had become slaves to the devil through sin and disobedience.

Now, through His death, Jesus had redeemed humanity from Satan's slave market of sin. Through His atonement, men and women could be united again with God.

God in perfect righteousness could not accept men and women in their sinful condition. Someone had to satisfy the penalty of the law. The apostle Paul wrote, *For the wages of sin is death, but the gift of God is eternal life in Christ Jesus our Lord (Romans 6:23).*

In Him we have redemption through His blood, the forgiveness of sins, according to the riches of His grace (Ephesians 1:7).

Paul further, wrote, *But God demonstrates His own love toward us, in that while we were still sinners, Christ died for us.*

Much more then, having now been justified by His blood, we shall be saved from wrath through Him (Romans 5:8,9).

Jesus, the sinless Son of God, shed His blood as the sacrifice to pay the penalty for the sins of humanity.

Now we can come boldly into the throne room of God. The blood of Jesus cleanses us from all sin. We too, can enter the Holy of Holies as priests.

Satan's hold over us has been broken. He has been overcome by the blood of the Lamb. Men and women can now be free from his dominion. Men and women, by the blood of Jesus, have been restored to their original place of authority.

All of Satan's work to destroy humanity, to separate them from God, to hold them in hopeless slavery to sin and death, has been completely overcome by one thing — the blood of Jesus.

When by faith we understand the power of the shed blood of Jesus, we know why Satan and demon powers are defeated and unable to touch us. When we acknowledge in faith, "the blood of Jesus," operating in our lives, we are actually covered and protected.

Through the shed blood of Jesus we have redemption, forgiveness and authority. We can walk in victory! We can continually demonstrate the truth — *And they overcame him* (Satan) *by the blood of the Lamb (Revelations 12:11a).*

Chapter Eight

God's Word, Alive and Powerful!

The curtains of eternity have just parted as we stand, looking over the shoulder of the apostle John. The intense loneliness of his exile on the Island of Patmos had suddenly been shattered by a heavenly vision. Satan and his demonic forces have poured out their hateful destruction on earth long enough. The King of kings and Lord of lords is preparing for His victorious return to earth.

Once again, we are told of a terrible battle in the spirit-world that will be fought in the future. It is the "end-time" confrontation between Jesus and all the forces of evil.

John wrote, *Then I saw heaven opened, and behold, a white horse. And He who sat on him was called Faithful and True, and in righteousness He judges and makes war.*

His eyes were like a flame of fire, and on His head were many crowns. He had a name written that no one knew except Himself.

He was clothed with a robe dipped in blood, and His name is called The Word of God (Revelation 19:11-13).

Picture the Son of God, His eyes flashing with fire, seated on a white horse with thousands of believers behind Him, also mounted on white horses.

This is the time for the final judgment of Satan and his followers.

Earlier in the book of Revelation, John revealed that we would overcome Satan by the blood of the Lamb and by the word of our testimony.

Now, through John's vision, we can look into the future and see the Son of God coming for Satan's final judgment. At this time, the evil forces will be totally overcome. Jesus will defeat Satan in this ultimate battle in the same way we are to defeat him in the everyday battles of life. Jesus is clothed with a vesture dipped in blood and He is using the Word of God as His only weapon.

Years before, when the apostle John wrote the book of John, he started that gospel with a description of the Word. *In the beginning was the Word, and the Word was with God, and the Word was God.* He made it even more definite when he stated, *And the Word became flesh and dwelt among us (John 1:1,14a).*

In the last book of the Bible, John, again revealed this truth about Jesus, *His name is called The Word of God.*

Continuing with this narrative, we are told, *And the armies in heaven, clothed in fine linen, white and clean, followed Him on white horses.*

Now out of His mouth goes a sharp sword, that with it He should strike the nations. And He Himself will rule them with a rod of iron. He Himself treads the winepress of the fierceness and wrath of Almighty God.

And He has on His robe and on His thigh a name written: KING OF KINGS AND LORD OF LORDS (Revelations 19:14-16).

The mighty weapon the Son of God has chosen to use in this all-important, final battle of the eternal conflict is the sword of the Spirit. It is the Word of God coming forth out of His mouth. The sword is not in the hands of Jesus — it is coming from His mouth. By speaking the Word of God, He will smite the nations and rule them; He will demonstrate His authority as the King of kings and the Lord of lords.

It is hard for us to picture a sword coming from the mouth. We have always seen it in someone's hand. Years ago, in Sunday school, I studied the armor of a Christian soldier. A large picture of this soldier hung on the bulletin board in the front of the classroom. Of course, he was young, strong and handsome. His armor was all in place. The shining shield had a bright crimson cross in the center and the large sword was held in his right hand ready for attack. Even as an adult, I continued to picture a Christian soldier that way.

During the days of the Jesus People Movement, I lived in Southern California. You always knew when you met one of this group because they carried the largest Bibles they could find. Many of them carried heavy Family Bibles. When I asked one young man why he needed a Bible that big, he answered, "That's my sword, Man!" He knew the power of Satan and he knew he needed a big sword!

That was much the way I pictured my sword. It was the Bible. It was God's Word. It should always be by my side, or in my hand. However, I found that was not enough. To be an overcomer, the sword has to come from my mouth.

When John described the climax of the end-time battle, he wrote that the beast and the false prophet were both cast into the lake of fire. Then, so that we would not be in any doubt about what John actually saw, he stated, *And the rest were killed with the sword which proceeded from the mouth of Him who sat on the horse (Revelation 19:21a).*

Satan has no problem when our sword of the Spirit is lying, gathering dust on a shelf. He does become concerned when he sees us studying the Bible and carrying it in our hands. However, he is not defeated until we speak the Word of God. When we speak it forth, God's Word becomes alive and powerful.

Our battles must be won by the Word of God, and that Word has to come out of our mouths, even as it will from the mouth of the victorious Lord Jesus as He returns to this earth.

Satan knows the power of the spoken word. In Revelation, John has written a description of Satan's present activities. *For the accuser of our brethren, who accused them before our God day and night, has been cast down (Revelation 12:10b).* The words coming from the mouth of Satan, both day and night, are accusations against us and our brethren. Satan is known as the accuser of the brethren.

Immediately, John saw we were not going to be defeated by the words coming from the mouth of Satan. He described us as overcomers! He knew the outcome when he wrote, *And they overcame him by the blood of the Lamb and by the word of their testimony (Revelation 12:11a).*

Is this passage in Revelation symbolic, or is it possible we can overcome and defeat Satan by speaking words out of our mouths? Can words become weapons in our warfare in the spirit?

The Bible says the weapons of our warfare are mighty through God to the pulling down of strongholds. Can mere words be mighty weapons?

Is it possible that when we discover the right words and begin to speak them, we will quit losing and start winning in the battles of life? If the answer is yes, if we can defeat Satan by using words alone, it is time we discover what these words are.

The "right words" were identified by John when he wrote, *And they overcame him by the blood of the Lamb and by the word of their testimony.* John said we were to overcome Satan by the Word of God, the "Logos" in our testimony.

When I think back to the struggles I have gone through in my life, I remember the frustration of what seemed an endless cycle of defeat. In my despair, I would reach out for sympathy and consolation from others. But the more I talked about the defeats, the more depressed I became.

The more I discussed my problems, the worse they seemed. I was overcome by my situations. I often spoke of my concerns for the economy and of the hopelessness of the future of the world. Continually, I discussed my problems in paying my bills. In the winter, I would tell friends I'd probably get the flu. I talked of how tired, weak and exhausted I felt. The more I talked, the worse things became.

Then, one day, I realized my testimony was full of my own negative words. I grasped the real meaning of the words, *And they overcame him by the blood of the Lamb and by the word of their testimony.* My weapon against my situations, against financial problems, against the winter flu, against the conditions in the world, and, ultimately, against Satan would be the "Logos," the "Word" in my testimony.

Instead of talking about what I could not do, I began to say, *"I can do all things through Christ who strengthens me (Philippians 4:13)."*

Instead of saying I could not pay my bills, I began to quote, *"My God shall supply all* [my] *needs according to His riches in glory by Christ Jesus (Philippians 4:19)."*

Instead of confessing I always caught the flu, I began to say, *"No evil shall befall* [me], *nor shall any plague come near* [my] *dwelling (Psalms 91:10)."*

Instead of discussing how bad the world situations were, I began to state, *"For whatever is born of God overcomes the world (1 John 5:4a),* and I am born of God!"

When I began to replace my own negative words with God's words in my testimony, I noticed that even while the situations remained unchanged, I was no longer depressed. As I continued to speak God's Word, my self-image began to change. I began to see myself as an overcomer, as a person who could do all things. I began to picture myself with all my needs supplied, as one walking in health instead of sickness. Although all the problems still existed, my mental attitude toward them began to change.

Gradually, something even more astonishing happened. I no longer had the flu several times each winter! I had money to pay my bills! I had favor and was successful in my job. God could even use me in the lives of those around me.

It was during this time I began to understand my battle had not been with the situations or with people. My struggles were not with flesh and blood, but were against Satan and his demonic forces.

When I spoke God's Word instead of speaking the problems, I knew something mighty was happening in the spirit world. Literally, I was overcoming Satan and his forces with the Word in my testimony. As the victory was won in the spirit world, the situations began to change in the natural world.

It is important for us to understand the power of the Word of God. How strong are the words that come out of His mouth? If we could speak the same words, would they have the same powerful results as when they were spoken by God?

To begin to understand the power of God's Words, let us turn our thoughts to the creation of our universe. This creation is the mightiest example of force we know. What were the building materials God used? What was the source of supply? What powerful energy was required to create planets, stars, galaxies and solar systems?

The writer of the book of Hebrews relates, *By faith we understand that the worlds were framed by the word of God, so that the things which are seen were not made of things which are visible (Hebrews 11:3).*

When God spoke, the universe came into existence. In the first chapter of Genesis, we read that God created by speaking words out of His mouth. Moses wrote, *Then God said ..., Then God said ..., Then God said ...,* Seven times we read the words, *Then God said....* Those words were the method of creation.

What happened when God said, *Let there be light?* How far did His voice travel? As God's voice traveled through the trillions of miles of the universe, did it gradually become weaker and weaker until it trailed off into nothingness?

Peter wrote, *the word of God which lives and abides forever (1 Peter 1:23b).*

Isaiah wrote, *it shall not return to Me void, but it shall accomplish what I please, and it shall prosper in the thing for which I sent it (Isaiah 55:11b).*

Job describes the voice of God as lightening. It travels at the speed of light; to the north one hundred and eighty-six thousand miles per second; to the south one hundred and eighty-six thousand miles per second; and the same to the east, and to the west.

Solar systems, galaxies and planets are still leaping into existence in all directions because of the words that came from God's mouth. The universe is expanding seven hundred and forty-four thousand miles per second by the power of the spoken Word of God.

No telescope ever designed by man will be able to discover the end of the universe, for the words spoken by God are still as strong and fast today as they were the first moment they came forth. They are God's words and they are alive and they are powerful.

I love the description of the voice of God given in Job, *At this also my heart trembles, and leaps from its place.*

Hear attentively the thunder of His voice, and the rumbling that comes from His mouth.

He sends it forth under the whole heaven, His lightning to the ends of the earth.

After it a voice roars; He thunders with His majestic voice, and He does not restrain them when His voice is heard.

God thunders marvelously with His voice; He does great things which we cannot comprehend (Job 37:1-5).

Jesus stood before the grave of Lazarus and He spoke three words, *Lazarus, Come Forth!* If Jesus had not called the name, "Lazarus," every grave would have emptied. He said, "Lazarus, come forth!" and Lazarus did. There was resurrection power in what Jesus spoke.

We do not accomplish great things by the amount of words we speak. Powerful things happen when we speak the Word of God in faith by the power of the Holy Spirit.

Until our faith has grown to the place that we can confidently speak God's Word regarding the situation we are facing, it is best to keep silent. If we are to experience the authority and power of that Word in our lives, we cannot speak negative words of unbelief. We must stop speaking our doubts. If we are to overcome Satan and walk in victory, we can do it only by speaking in faith.

Faith comes by reading, meditating on, and hearing the Word of God. When we meditate and visualize the great results of God's truth in our situation, our faith will begin to grow. When we begin to speak God's Word, confidently and boldly, mighty things will happen.

When the children of Israel came into the Promised Land, the Lord opened the Jordan River and they were able to walk across on dry land. However, just after they had walked through this miracle, they faced the heavily fortified city of Jericho. This city guarded the entrance to the land and had a very strong army. The walls were high and wide, and the huge gates were closed. God's people were faced with their first battle in their new land.

God had miraculously parted the Jordan River, but on this occasion, He gave Joshua strange instructions. Joshua was to form a procession of seven priests blowing on ram's horns, followed by priests bearing the ark of the covenant, with the men of war marching last. For six days they were to march once around the city, and then on the seventh day, they were to march around the city seven times.

God also said that on the seventh day, after they had encompassed the city seven times, *Then it shall come to pass, when they make a long blast with the ram's horn, and when you hear the sound of the trumpet, that all the people shall shout with a great shout; then the wall of the city will fall down flat. And the people shall go up every man straight before him (Joshua 6:5).*

God gave another very definite, strong command about this march that was to last for seven days. *You shall not shout or make any noise with your voice, nor shall any word proceed out of your mouth, until the day I say to you, 'Shout!' Then you shall shout (Joshua 6:10b).*

I wonder what the priests and soldiers were thinking when they marched around the walls.

Forty years previously the spies had brought back a report of the strength of this land and of the size of the men. *The land through which we have gone as spies is a land that devours its inhabitants, and all the people whom we saw in it are men of a great stature.*

There we saw the giants (the descendants of Anak came from the giants); and we were like grasshoppers in our own sight, and so we were in their sight (Numbers 13:32b,33).

For six days, the Israelites marched completely around those walls. They must have studied them carefully, looking for a weak place. Instead, they saw how high and strong they were on every side.

Have you ever wondered why they were instructed not to speak? Probably, being human just like you and I, they would have begun to discuss the evil reports they had received concerning the strength of that land.

"I wonder how tall those men really are; are we really like grasshoppers to them?" they might have asked.

"What did our spies mean years ago, when they said this land devours its inhabitants?"

Perhaps they would have begun to discuss how impossible it was for them to take the city. "Look at the size of those walls. We have nothing that will help us scale them. I haven't seen a crack anywhere."

"We're not prepared to meet an army of this size."

"I thought God said He was going to give us this land. Why should we fight to take it?"

But there was no negative conversation, for God had commanded them not to shout, not to make any noise, and not even to say one word. For seven long days, the only sound to be heard was the marching of thousands of feet on the sand and the trumpets of the seven priests giving praise to God.

Finally, on the seventh time around the city on the seventh day, Joshua shouted, *Shout; for the Lord has given you the city.*

You know the end of the story. At that tremendous shout, the walls fell down and the city was defeated.

When we read about a miracle, it seems so easy. But have you ever wondered what the children of Israel might have been thinking during the seven days they waited for God to work?

Did any of these instructions make sense? For six days did anything seem to change? Did the walls start to crumble?

On the seventh day, when they started marching early in the morning so they could make it around that great city seven times, did anything seem different than on the first day?

In the late afternoon, when they had marched six times around the walls, and their feet were burning and their bodies were tired, did anything seem different?

Were God's instructions going to work?

It must have seemed they had been trying God's way for a long time! It would have been easy to doubt and complain. However, God's timing was perfect, and obedience to His Word brought victory.

The battle had been won in the Spirit and not in the flesh. It had been won by obedience to God. The obvious course of action would have been to use their natural weapons. However, God wanted His people to know who the real enemy was. He wanted them to recognize where the real warfare was taking place. God wanted His people to learn how to use spiritual weapons to pull down the strongholds of the enemy.

Paul wrote about this: *For though we walk in the flesh, we do not war according to the flesh. For the weapons of our warfare are not carnal but mighty in God for pulling down strongholds (2 Corinthians 10:3,4).*

Isaiah wrote, *"For My thoughts are not your thoughts, nor are your ways My ways," says the Lord. "For as the heavens are higher than the earth, so are My ways higher than your ways, and My thoughts than your thoughts.*

"For as the rain comes down, and the snow from heaven, and do not return there, but water the earth, and make it bring forth and bud, that it may give seed to the sower, and bread to the eater, So shall My word be that goes forth from My mouth; it shall not return to Me void, but it shall accomplish what I please, and

it shall prosper in the thing for which I sent it (Isaiah 55:8-11)."

We don't need to understand God's thoughts. We are incapable of knowing them. Our part is to believe that when His Word is spoken, it will not return void. It will accomplish that which He pleases. It shall prosper in the thing whereto it was sent.

We send the Word by speaking it, and when we speak God's Word, it cannot return void. It must accomplish the things that it was sent to accomplish. When we speak His Word to the situations, to the trials and testings in our lives, they will change.

When Satan tries to rob us of our finances, we must not talk as we have in the past about how bad the economy is and how we cannot afford to pay our bills. Instead, we will speak the Word of God. *My God shall supply all* [my] *needs according to his riches in glory by Christ Jesus.*

When sickness and disease come against us, we will speak what His Word says about sickness and disease. *I am the Lord your God that heals you. By my stripes you are healed. I will take sickness and disease out of the midst of thee.*

We will no longer talk about our various illnesses and about how terrible we feel. Instead we will speak the Word of God.

Solomon wrote, *There is one who speaks like the piercings of a sword, but the tongue of the wise promotes health (Proverbs 12:18).* When we speak words of health, those words release health into our bodies and into those around us.

Solomon also wrote, *Death and life are in the power of the tongue, and those who love it will eat its fruit (Proverbs 18:21).* When we speak words of sickness and death, it releases the power of sickness and death to work in our lives. When we speak words of life from the Word of God, we have the power of that life. We will die or live by whether we choose to speak the written Word of God.

Paul wrote, *But the righteousness of faith speaks in this way, ...*

The word is near you, even in your mouth and in your heart (that is, the word of faith which we preach): that if you confess with your mouth the Lord Jesus and believe in your heart that God has raised Him from the dead, you will be saved.

For with the heart one believes to righteousness, and with the mouth confession is made to salvation (Romans 10:6a,8,10).

When we meditate on the Word, we receive it into our hearts. However, the power of the Word is not released until we begin to speak it.

David knew the angels were moved into action on his behalf when he began to speak the Word of God. He wrote, *Bless the Lord, you His angels, Who excel in strength, who do His word, Heeding the voice of His word (Psalms 103:20).* Later he wrote, *He sent His word and healed them, And delivered them from their destructions (Psalms 107:20).*

God created us in His own image to be just like Himself. God is a creator, and He creates by speaking. We are also creators. We create by speaking words from our mouths. We either create evil by speaking doubt and unbelief, or we create good by speaking God's Word in faith. When we speak His Word in faith, it has the same powerful results as if the Creator God were saying it Himself.

When you absorb the Word of God into your spirit, and go forth and speak it from your mouth in faith and by the power of the Holy Spirit, you are going to subdue kingdoms as Joshua and the children of Israel did. You are going to tear down the rulers of the darkness over the cities of this world and over the nations of this world. You are going to restore the kingdom of God everywhere you go.

You are going to hold your head high and go forth with boldness, for when you go, the Word of God will be with you as a sharp, two-edged sword coming forth out of your mouth. It will subdue kingdoms. It will tear down strongholds. It will bring to nought the works of the devil and it will demonstrate his defeat.

Chapter Nine

Speak the Word Only

Great crowds had gathered to hear Jesus teach on a beautiful hillside at the north edge of the Sea of Galilee. The people had heard about the miracles Jesus performed, but when they heard Him teach, they were even more amazed. He didn't talk as their religious leaders did. Instead, Jesus taught with authority and power.

For years, the people had heard a message of guilt and condemnation. They were held in bondage by what had become an empty religion. Now Jesus had come and His words were of life and hope. He said that God, the Father, loved them. He taught them how they could be blessed. He spoke the good news — they could be free from bondage, torment, and the oppression of the devil.

A centurion had been stationed in Galilee with his regiment to keep peace in that area. Although he was a powerful Roman military leader, he had a tenderness toward the things of God and love for the nation of Israel. For we read in the seventh chapter of Luke that he was responsible for building the Jewish synagogue in Capernaum.

This Roman was responsible to his government for everything that happened in Galilee and when he heard of this large gathering, he must have sent some of his soldiers to discover what was happening. The

119

report that Jesus was teaching with authority may have alarmed him at first, but when he heard Jesus' message of love, hope, and blessing, his concern must have been relieved. Then reports began to come back about the healings which Jesus performed.

This centurion had a servant who was paralyzed and was being tormented by demons to the point of death. When he heard about the miracles Jesus did, he began to wonder if Jesus could heal his servant. Then word came that Jesus was coming toward Capernaum, and the centurion sent the elders of the city to ask Jesus to come and heal his servant. Jesus started toward the centurion's home.

Although he was respected by the Jewish people in Capernaum, the centurion knew that most religious leaders considered Romans as unworthy dogs. Jesus didn't know him. His house would be considered "unclean" by the Jews. Why would Jesus come to his house?

Suddenly, the answer came. He knew how his servant could be healed. He would go to Jesus. When he approached Jesus, he said, *"Lord, my servant is lying at home paralyzed, dreadfully tormented."*

And Jesus said to him, "I will come and heal him."

The centurion answered and said, "Lord, I am not worthy that You should come under my roof. But only speak a word, and my servant will be healed.

"For I also am a man under authority, having soldiers under me. And I say to this one, 'Go,' and he goes; and to another, 'Come,' and he comes; and to my servant, 'Do this,' and he does it."

When Jesus heard it, He marveled, and said to those who followed, "Assuredly, I say to you, I have not found such great faith, not even in Israel!"

Then Jesus said to the centurion, "Go your way; and as you have believed, so let it be done for you."

And his servant was healed that same hour (Matthew 8:6-10,13).

This centurion, a military man, understood authority. He was under authority, and he also had soldiers under his authority. Even as he obeyed orders from Rome, he controlled the men in his command by the orders that he gave. Because he understood authority in the natural realm, he could understand authority in the spiritual realm. Because he understood spiritual authority, he could say, *Speak the word only, and my servant shall be healed (KJV).*

By speaking the Word of God, we can release words of healing. We can speak words of deliverance. We can speak words of prosperity and blessing. We can speak words of peace in the family relationships.

The faith of this Roman soldier prompted Jesus to say, *I have not found such great faith, not even in Israel!*

Notice that the centurion said, *Speak the word only.* How often after speaking the Word of God, people go on to speak the problem. How often they say, "I know God can heal, but so many people are dying of this disease today."

"I know God wants me to prosper, but the economy is so bad, it's just hard to get ahead these days."

"I know God wants me to live in peace, but my husband (or wife) just wants to argue all the time."

"I know God wants to bless my business, but the competition makes it impossible for me to keep growing."

If we are to walk in authority and understand authority, we must learn to speak the Word only, as the centurion did. We must no longer speak the problem, but continually declare God's Word.

As with the centurion, those who walk in true authority are people who have love and compassion for others. They have learned how to give and bless others. Those who really understand authority are not proud and arrogant. Instead, they are humble and consider the needs of others over themselves. They also understand authority because they are under authority.

We can only understand and live in authority when we accept the authority and lordship of God over every area of our lives. We, like Jesus, will love people, but will hate the devil and his demon powers. We will humbly, but confidently, realize that it's not our words, but the authority of speaking God's Words that brings the victory.

Jesus overcame Satan in the wilderness at the beginning of His ministry by saying, *It is written.* At each temptation, He spoke the Word of God, and Satan was overcome because of the Word in the testimony of Jesus.

Jesus cast out the demon spirits and healed the sick by speaking. Matthew wrote, *When evening had come, they brought to Him many who were demon-*

possessed. *And He cast out the spirits with a word, and healed all who were sick (Matthew 8:16).*

In Luke we read, *And they were astonished at His teaching, for His word was with authority.* When Jesus taught, he taught with authority and power.

Now in the synagogue there was a man who had a spirit of an unclean demon. And he cried out with a loud voice, saying, "Let us alone! What have we to do with You, Jesus of Nazareth? Did You come to destroy us? I know You, who You are—the Holy One of God!"

But Jesus rebuked him, saying, "Be quiet, and come out of him!" And when the demon had thrown him in their midst, it came out of him and did not hurt him.

So they were all amazed and spoke among themselves, saying, "What a word this is! For with authority and power He commands the unclean spirits, and they come out (Luke 4:32-36)."

The Word Jesus taught astonished and amazed those who heard it because it was with authority and power. Even the demon spirits had to obey.

One day, when Jesus was on the shores of the Sea of Galilee, a great multitude gathered, and Jesus entered into a boat and began to teach the parable of the sower and the seed. Mark gives us this account of the parable of the sower in the forth chapter of Mark.

Listen! Behold, a sower went out to sow.

And it happened, as he sowed, that some seed fell by the wayside; and the birds of the air came and devoured it.

Jesus went on to describe the seed that fell on the stony ground, the seed that fell among thorns, and the seed that fell on good ground, gave fruit, sprang up and increased. When Jesus was explaining the parable to his disciples, He told them, *The sower sows the word.* The seed which Jesus was talking about was the Word of God.

He went on to say, *And these are the ones by the wayside where the word is sown. And when they hear, Satan comes immediately and takes away the word that was sown in their hearts.*

The fowl of the air is a picture of Satan and how he comes immediately to steal the Word of God after it's sown in hearts. Satan desires to rob believers of many things, but his primary goal is to steal the seed of the Word, because he knows the power of that Word.

Jesus continued, *These likewise are the ones sown on stony ground who, when they hear the word, immediately receive it with gladness; and they have no root in themselves, and so endure only for a time. Afterward, when tribulation or persecution arises for the word's sake, immediately they stumble.*

Have you ever heard the expression, "After every mountain-top experience, there comes a valley"? For years we thought this was true. It seemed like every time we were in a wonderful conference and learned new things from the Lord, we would have a terrible time the next few days, or even weeks.

We didn't understand what was happening in the spirit world, and so we weren't able to stand against it. We thought life, in the spirit, was made up of mountains and valleys. We thought we were submissively to accept tribulations and persecutions as

God's dealing in our lives because God wanted us to learn something.

Finally, we realized what Jesus meant in this parable. Jesus said that after the Word is sown, Satan would come to steal it. The word may be sown in a good conference, seminar, sermon, class, or in our personal Bible study. Then, when the tribulations and persecutions come, we should not stumble or become "offended" (KJV).

Satan's major goal is to steal the Word that is sown before it has time to take root.

The "valleys" we were accepting as from God, were the tribulations and persecutions that came "for the Word's sake." It was Satan who was bringing adversity against us as his strategy to rob us.

Nearly two thousand years ago, Jesus warned the disciples of this. He knew Satan would come to steal the Word and that immediately some would be offended. He knew that if they let themselves be offended, Satan could steal the seed of the Word.

Satan's strategy for robbing us of a newly revealed truth is still to bring affliction and persecution "for the Word's sake." What happened immediately after Jesus taught the disciples the Parable of the Sower and the Seeds in the forth chapter of Mark?

On the same day, when evening had come, He said to them, "Let us cross over to the other side."

Now when they had left the multitude, they took Him along in the boat as He was. And other little boats were also with Him.

And a great windstorm arose, and the waves beat into the boat, so that it was already filling.

But He was in the stern, asleep on a pillow. And they awoke Him and said to Him, "Teacher, do You not care that we are perishing?"

Then He arose and rebuked the wind, and said to the sea, "Peace, be still!" And the wind ceased and there was a great calm.

But He said to them, "Why are you so fearful? How is it that you have no faith?"

And they feared exceedingly, and said to one another, "Who can this be, that even the wind and the sea obey Him!"

Jesus had been teaching all day. He had been sowing the seed of the Word, and just like Jesus had told them in the parable, Satan had come immediately to take away that Word. Tribulation and persecution came in the form of a great storm of wind and waves beating into the ship.

This was an opportunity for the disciples to act on what Jesus had been teaching. Instead, they stumbled and became offended. They anxiously awakened Jesus and fearfully questioned, *Teacher, do you not care that we are perishing?* They had become offended just as Jesus had warned them not to do.

When Jesus awoke, He didn't join the disciples in their desperate struggle to bail out the ship. He didn't grab an oar to help hold the bow against the wind. Jesus stood up in the tossing boat, in the midst of the storm, and began to speak. He began to talk to the wind and to the sea. He spoke words out of His mouth. He said, *Peace, be still.* The wind ceased and there was a great calm.

In the stillness following that great turbulence, Jesus turned to the disciples and asked, *Why are you so fearful? How is it that you have no faith?*

It should be no surprise to us, that every time God reveals a new truth to us from His Word, testings come in that area. We immediately have an opportunity to prove that truth and make it real in our lives, or to become offended.

When God first revealed this truth to me, of how I could walk in divine health, testing came against my body. Never before had I experienced so many symptoms. I would stand up, double over in pain, and Satan would whisper, "Cancer." Terrible fear would try to enter my mind. I could either prove God's Word, or I could run to the doctor in fear. I would make myself stand erect, and I would begin to quote Scripture. Over a period of time, the afflictions left.

When I discovered the truth of how all of the blessings of Abraham now belonged to me, and how I was to walk in divine provision and prosperity, immediately there were storms that came against my finances. I lost my job, went three months without work, and then took a job at half my previous income. It was during this time God moved us into the big house in Anaheim Hills. The trials and persecutions came, but God gave us His provision and prosperity.

In every area of our lives, when the truth of God's Word is sown in our hearts and revealed as the answer to our needs, we find Satan bringing storms in an attempt to cause us to become resentful and to stop believing God's Word.

James put it this way, *My brethren, count it all joy when you fall into various trials, knowing that the testing of your faith produces patience. But let patience have its perfect work, that you may be perfect and complete, lacking nothing (James 1:2-4).*

Perhaps it would be easy to say, "I tried God's Word. I believed it. It just didn't work for me."

Often when we are out on the sea of life, the storms against us are so great that it does seem we are about to sink. It would be easy for us to ask, as the disciples did, "Teacher, don't You even care that we're perishing?"

We cry, "Lord, you promised in your Word You would meet all our needs according to your riches in glory by Christ Jesus, but I'm sick. I can't pay my bills. Don't you care?"

The moment we become offended, Satan is able to steal the seed of the Word out of our hearts. We will either lose God's Word or we will stand up in the storms of life and begin to prove His Word so that the seed can mature and bring forth fruit.

To the storms of sickness, we should speak God's Words of healing. To the storms of finances, we should speak God's Words for provision and blessing. To the storms of oppression, we should speak God's Words of deliverance. To the storms of doubt, we should speak God's Words of faith.

John wrote, *I write to you, fathers, because you have known Him who is from the beginning. I write to you, young men, because you have overcome the wicked one. I write to you, little children, because you have known the Father.*

I have written to you, fathers, because you have known Him who is from the beginning. I have written to you, young men, because you are strong, and the word of God abides in you, and you have overcome the wicked one (1 John 2:13,14).

The young men John wrote to were men who had overcome the wicked one. They weren't losers; they were winners. They were overcomers, and John wrote the reason for their success. It was because the Word of God "abided" in them.

When Satan came immediately to steal the seed of the Word, they didn't become offended. They spoke the Word of God. His Word had remained in them and they overcame the wicked one.

My parent's home is surrounded by huge towering oak trees. Their giant, spreading limbs and foliage provide dense shade for the house and the yard. These oaks weren't always the giant trees they are today. I grew up in that house, and I remember when they were small trees. Before that time, each tree had begun as a small seed, an acorn, lying in the ground. I'm sure there was a time when someone looking at that ground could have said, "There's no oak tree here." However, as the seed remained in the soil, and as the rain and the sunshine came, that seed began to sprout and grow.

Over the years, those oaks have gone through many seasons. The spring rains, the summer heat, the fall winds, and the long, cold winters have all contributed to the growth of those trees. Over the years, they have survived, even as hurricanes have swept through the area. These storms have made the roots of the trees go deeper into the soil. Today they stand, giant overcomers of the storms of life.

So it is when we speak God's Word. Sometimes we see no immediate signs of life or change in our situation. We know the storms will come as Satan attempts to steal the Word from our hearts. However, when we allow the seed to remain and grow in an atmosphere of faith, our roots will go down deeper into the soil of God's love.

David wrote about a tree in the first Psalm. He described a person who delights in the Word of God. *He shall be like a tree Planted by the rivers of water, That brings forth its fruit in its season, Whose leaf also shall not wither; And whatever he does shall prosper (Psalm 1:3).*

If our lives are to be like a tree, bringing forth fruit with leaves that do not wither, we must allow God's truths to remain in our hearts. We must determine that we will not allow Satan to steal the seed of the Word from our lives. We must determine that despite the storms of adversity, we will continue to meditate on the Scriptures both day and night and to speak those words.

The writer of the book of Hebrews states, *For the word of God is living and powerful, and sharper than any two-edged sword, piercing even to the division of soul and spirit, and of joints and marrow, and is a discerner of the thoughts and intents of the heart (Hebrews 4:12).*

The Word of God is alive, and it's powerful! We shouldn't be intimidated by the power of the devil. We have the power of the living Word of God and that power is released when we speak it forth.

Often having received, meditated on, and spoken God's Word regarding situations in our life, we look around in the time of testing that comes, and we see no change.

Then Satan brings thoughts to our minds. "It didn't work. Nothing has happened." He will say, "You need to get a lawyer and fight this thing," or, "You are going to need surgery." In today's economy, he may say, "You are going to be forced into bankruptcy." You may hear, "You are going to get a divorce and end your marriage."

We may be tempted to reply, "I tried believing God's Word, I tried believing and speaking His promises, but nothing happened."

That isn't the truth. The writer of the book of Hebrews tells us the Word of God is alive and powerful. God's Word is the truth. If we, in spite of the storms of life, keep on believing, keep on meditating, and keep on speaking the Word of God in the power of the Holy Spirit, we will see God's Word come forth to calm that storm.

Mark wrote about an incident involving another tree, a fig tree. We can learn much about the authority of speaking God's Word when we consider this event *(Mark 11:12-14,20-23)*.

Now the next day, when they had come out from Bethany, He was hungry. And seeing from afar a fig tree having leaves, He went to see if perhaps He would find something on it. And when He came to it, He found nothing but leaves, for it was not the season for figs.

In response Jesus said to it, "Let no one eat fruit from you ever again." And His disciples heard it.

The disciples heard Jesus talking to a fig tree. He was speaking with authority just as He had on the Sea of Galilee when he stood in the boat. Jesus spoke to the fig tree and then they went on their way, *Now in the morning, as they passed by, they saw the fig tree dried up from the roots.*

When Jesus spoke to the storm, everything changed in an instant, but when He spoke to the fig tree, the disciples didn't see any change until the next day. If some of us had spoken to that fig tree, we would have watched it and when we saw the leaves were still green, we would have said, "Well, I guess it didn't work."

Jesus didn't wait to see a change. He spoke to the fig tree and He knew what was going to happen. We cannot measure the success of the Word of God by what we see. When we pray for a person and curse the cancer within him, we speak the Word of God in faith. We know the Word has accomplished the thing that it was sent to do. The human body must begin to conform to the Word that was sent into that body.

So Jesus answered and said to them, "Have faith in God." We must have faith that will speak the Word, and even if seeing no change, will go on believing, and will come back later to see the results. We must have faith that will keep on believing until the Word is manifested.

Jesus continued, *For assuredly, I say to you, whoever says to this mountain, 'Be removed and be cast into the sea,' and does not doubt in his heart, but believes that those things he says will come to pass, he will have whatever he says.* The key word is "says." It's not enough to believe in our heart. We must say it! We must be like Jesus with the two-edged sword coming forth from our mouth.

Jesus talked to the sea, He talked to the fig tree, and He instructed His disciples to talk to the mountain!

In our life, we have mountains of circumstances, problems, and situations. What did Jesus tell us to say to these mountains?

We are to speak the Word of God so that it can come forth as a two-edged sword from our mouth. *Be removed and be cast into the sea.*

We must have the kind of faith that comes by hearing the Word of God. The apostle Paul wrote, *So then faith comes by hearing, and hearing by the word of God* (Romans 10:17).

The original Greek word translated "word" in this verse in not the general word "Logos," but "rhema" which is the specific "word" that God has spoken to us by His Holy Spirit. It is His promise to us, personally, regarding the situation we are in.

It is important that before we begin to "confess" the general "Logos" Word of God, we take time to listen to God and hear from Him the specific "rhema" that He speaks to our hearts regarding our personal situation. It is this "rhema" that will release our faith.

Many Christians have been wounded in their faith because they have tried to "confess" a scripture to satisfy their own desires without taking the time necessary to first hear from God and receive His specific Word in answer to their need.

It is important to take time to read, study and meditate on all the "Logos," or general promises, regarding our specific need. Then, we must listen to the Holy Spirit and ask Him to give us His personal "Word" for our need. As we do, God will quicken a specific "rhema" to our spirits and at that moment, faith will leap into existence.

We will say, "Yes! This is God's promise to me!" Then, we will begin to speak or "declare" that Word through the faith which has come alive within our spirits.

We must have the kind of faith that not only believes the Word, but speaks the Word. The faith that rises up within us and shouts, "No, Devil! No plague shall come near our dwelling! These symptoms must leave."

When Satan attacks our finances, what will we say? "Our God shall supply all our needs, not according to the measure of our needs, but according to the measure of His riches in glory by Christ Jesus."

The devil says, "You are going to fail. You are going to be a failure."

Our reply should be, "I can do all things through Christ who strengthens me"; or "I am more than a conqueror through him that loved me and gave himself for me."

Remember, Jesus spoke to the fig tree and it looked just the same. We are to speak God's Word in faith as we are led and empowered by the Holy Spirit.

Then, either instantly or progressively, we will have what we say.

Isaiah made it clear. When we keep on believing and speaking what God has spoken to us through His Word, we will without fail, see that Word accomplished in our lives. He wrote, *For as the rain comes down, and the snow from heaven, and do not return there, but water the earth, and make it bring forth and bud, that it may give seed to the sower and bread to the eater, so shall My word be that goes forth from My mouth; it shall not return to Me void, but it shall accomplish what I please, and it shall prosper in the thing for which I sent it (Isaiah 55:10-11).*

We send it by speaking the Word that God has revealed to us . That Word cannot fail or return void. It will always prosper as it accomplishes its intended purpose in our lives.

Chapter Ten

The Name Above Every Name

"I am going to kill you!" the hitchhiker shouted as he pointed his gun at Johnny Rutledge.

It was a warm summer evening and Johnny had stopped for a traffic light on his way home. Two young men came running over to the car. One was using a crutch, and as they quickly opened the doors and climbed into the car, he mumbled something about being in terrible pain. They were already in the car when they asked for a ride to their home just a few blocks down the street and off the main road. Johnny knew he was in a terrible situation!

When he stopped the car where they said, the two men jumped out. Suddenly, one of the men turned and Johnny found himself looking down the barrel of a stub-nose revolver. "Get out of the car!" snapped the man.

They demanded his money and when they discovered he had only a few dollars, the gunman's eyes flashed and he snarled, "That's not enough! For that small amount, I'm going to kill you!"

Johnny was still staring at the gun when he heard the words, "You're going to die, right now." The other man moved quickly out of the way.

Suddenly words were coming from Johnny's lips, "In the name of Jesus, you can't shoot me!" he stated. Confidence came over Johnny as he repeated those words, "In the name of Jesus, you can't shoot me!" Then with even greater boldness and authority, he started repeating "In the name of Jesus! In the name of Jesus! In the name of Jesus!"

"Wait a minute! Let me check him out!" the second robber said. Going through his pockets, he found some change, his knife and then his watch.

"Get away so I can shoot!" yelled the gunman.

"No, wait, let's check his car."

Johnny continued to repeat, "In the name of Jesus, you can't shoot me!"

Looking into the car, the man saw Johnny's Bible. Jumping back, he exclaimed, "Hey, this guy's for real. He's a Jesus man. We can't shoot a Jesus man."

Johnny was still repeating, "In the name of Jesus," when the gunman told him to get back in his car and take off.

Johnny drove away from what could easily have been the site of his death, and he was completely unharmed. He filed a police report and the men soon were taken into custody. They had directed Johnny to within a few houses of where they were staying. Their obvious intention was that Johnny would never leave there alive.

What power was released when Johnny said, "In the name of Jesus?" How could merely saying these words turn a pending tragedy into triumph?

First, we must understand that our spirit-enemies are afraid of the name of Jesus. Moses said, *Then all peoples of the earth shall see that you are called by the name of the Lord, and they shall be afraid of you (Deuteronomy 28:10).*

Next, we should realize that calling the name "Jesus" brings salvation. Paul wrote, *For whoever calls upon the name of the Lord shall be saved (Romans 10:13).* Johnny called upon the name of the Lord Jesus, and he was saved from death.

When a person calls upon the name of the Lord, the Bible says that he "shall be," not "might be," saved. First, he's saved from sin. Then, he can be saved from danger, from sickness, from oppression, and from poverty. He can be saved from Satan's plans to kill, steal and destroy by calling on the name of the Lord.

What is the name of the Lord? What name are we to use?

The angel of the Lord appeared to Mary and told her, *You will conceive in your womb and bring forth a Son, and shall call His name Jesus (Luke 1:31).* The name "Jesus," means "Savior," or "God save us." When we in faith say "Jesus," we are recognizing Him as the One who can save us. We have uttered a prayer that releases God's power. We have said, "God save us!"

After Peter healed the lame man, he was asked, *By what power or by what name have you done this?*

He replied, *Let it be known to you all, and to all the people of Israel, that by the name of Jesus Christ of Nazareth, whom you crucified, whom God raised from the dead, by Him this man stands here before you whole.*

He went on to state, *Nor is there salvation in any other, for there is no other name under heaven given among men by which we must be saved (Acts 4:7,10,12).*

139

Paul agreed when he wrote, *Therefore God also has highly exalted Him and given Him the name which is above every name, that at the name of Jesus every knee should bow, of those in heaven, and of those on earth, and of those under the earth, and that every tongue should confess that Jesus Christ is Lord, to the glory of God the Father (Philippians 2:9-11).*

The church lost much of its authority when it stopped using the name of Jesus. Some religious leaders began to think it would be more acceptable and less offensive to the world if we called Jesus, "The Master, The Prophet, The Teacher," or "The Man Upstairs."

Over forty years ago, my mother taught the small children in the Sunday school of a denominational church where we were members. One day, the pastor and Sunday school superintendent came to her and said, "Don't use the name Jesus when teaching the children. It will confuse their little minds. Just talk about God and love. Never use the name Jesus."

Years ago, when Joyce and I were ministering in the Philippines, we attended the First Asian Ecumenical Conference. It had been called by President Marcos, and included the top leaders of the Eastern religions from all over Asia and the "top Christian leaders" of the Philippines. The meeting was being televised all over Asia, and Joyce and I were the only Americans there.

We had come to this meeting with a well-known Filipino evangelist who was attending the conference in the hopes of renewing a friendship with the man who was now President Marcos' Executive Secretary.

He was also Secretary of Civil Service and the most politically powerful man in the Philippines next to the President. My friend had known him several years before and we were praying that God would give us an opening so that the evangelist could have a word with him.

When we parked our jeep in the town where the meeting was being held, we were honored as Americans and invited to the Mayor's home for lunch. As we entered his home, we saw a man seated alone at the table. It was the Executive Secretary. When he turned to see who had come in and saw the evangelist whom he immediately recognized and Americans, he invited us to sit with him.

After he and the evangelist had exchanged greetings, he turned to Joyce and myself and we began to talk about Jesus. We told him of the love that we had for the people of the Philippines. We told him about the meetings where hundreds had received Jesus as their Savior. We described miracles that had happened the night before. We were excited about a Jesus who was still alive and doing the same works today as He did two thousand years ago. We knew Jesus was still the answer to every need in the lives of the people of the Philippines.

He was obviously moved, and he began to share with us how years before he had taught Sunday school in his church. He told us that at one time the church had been an important part of his life, but later, when he became involved in other things, his interest had dwindled. He said, "I felt I had learned all they had to teach me."

When we stood to leave the table and go into the conference where he was to speak as President Marcos' representative, he shook my hand and said, "Your being here has given me the inspiration to say what I am going to say to the religious leaders in this conference."

We went into the conference and each of the religious leaders and their groups took the platform and did chants, burned incense, or rang bells in worship of their gods. Joyce and I sat silently binding the power of Satan and of those religious, demon spirits.

When the "Christian" religious leaders from the Philippines came to the front, they didn't even mention the name of Jesus. Joyce and I felt such grief within our spirits. "Father, isn't the name of Jesus even going to be mentioned?" we cried silently.

After all the religious leaders had spoken, and a prayer had been read, we continued to pray as the Mayor and the Governor greeted the people. We then stood and cheered with all the people when the Executive Secretary was introduced. He introduced the evangelist, Joyce and myself to the congress, and then with the eyes of the whole Eastern world watching by television, he began to speak.

After a few introductory words about unity, he said, "I noticed when the religious leaders came to join in reading the prayer something was left out. "Did anyone else notice what it was?" he asked, as he looked directly at us.

"You left out the words, 'In the name of Jesus'," he stated, to the shock of the religious leaders.

He continued, "Now, I assume this prayer was prepared by a committee, and these words were left out in the interest of unity, but we, as Christians, must never do that. We must agree to disagree, but in our disagreement work together for unity of purpose and understanding.

"We as Christians must never deny the name of Jesus, for it's Jesus who is the center of our whole purpose, life and message to the world!"

What joy we felt when we heard the name of Jesus being magnified in that important conference by the most important person there! Even with the joy we felt, we had no idea of the magnitude of what the Lord was doing.

At that time, there was concern in many foreign countries that missionaries were agents of the Central Intelligence Agency. That morning, just after we had left for the conference, President Marcos had issued an edict that all foreign missionaries must leave the Philippines within thirty days. At the time we were there, the Philippines was under martial law and an edict was an immediate law.

When we arrived back in Manila that evening, we found missionaries and other Christian workers gathered in distress at the hotel. They had spent most of the day praying for divine intervention.

We didn't know what had happened for many months, but that edict was never mentioned again. The missionaries were allowed to stay.

The following year, when we were talking to one of the missionaries from Manila, we told her about this meeting. She laughed and shook her head, "You don't even know what happened!

"The Executive Secretary was probably the only one who could have changed that edict. God put it on the heart of the evangelist to attend that meeting and to take you with him. Most of the Filipino people love Americans and God used you to lift up the name of Jesus, and the course of a nation was changed."

Jesus has given every believer the legal right to use His name.

In the United States, we can write words and place numbers on a piece of paper, called a check. When we sign our name to that check, it gives the person we made the check payable to the legal right to go to our bank and demand the amount of money we have written. By writing our name on the check, we have given them legal authority to withdraw the funds from our account.

On one occasion, when I was the Executive Vice-President of an organization, the President was out of town much of the time traveling. We were in the midst of negotiations on some valuable property. There were others trying to buy the same property, and we knew that when it was time to sign the papers, the person selling the property wouldn't wait.

The President of the organization filled out a legal paper, called a "Power of Attorney," which gave me the legal right to sign his name in his absence. With that "Power of Attorney," my signature would be just as legally binding as his own. It would have the same legal authority as if the President had signed himself.

Jesus has given us His name. He has given us a "Power of Attorney" to use His name. When we use His name, it has the same effect as if Jesus were doing it Himself.

If Jesus were to ask the Father for something, would He give it to Him? When we ask in Jesus' name, will our heavenly Father give it to us?

If Jesus laid hands on the sick today, would they recover? Jesus said they would if we would do it in His name *(Mark 16:17,18)*. It would have the same effect as if Jesus were standing there doing it Himself.

Matthew told us about our "Power of Attorney." *Then Jesus came and spoke to them, saying, "All authority has been given to Me in heaven and on earth.*

"Go therefore and make disciples of all the nations, baptizing them in the name of the Father and of the Son and of the Holy Spirit, teaching them to observe all things that I have commanded you; and lo, I am with you always, even to the end of the age (Matthew 28:18-20)."

All power — all authority — was given to Jesus in heaven and on earth. In that same power, we are to go, teach, and baptize "in the name of the Father, of the Son, and of the Holy Ghost."

Luke describes how the disciples felt when they first experienced that power. *Then the seventy returned with joy, saying, "Lord, even the demons are subject to us in Your name (Luke 10:17)."*

The disciples had gone out to minister and they had used the name of Jesus. They were so excited when they returned that they could hardly wait to tell

Jesus. "Lord, the devils are subject to us through your name! It was just as though you were there yourself."

Jesus replied, *And He said to them, "I saw Satan fall like lightning from heaven.*

"Behold, I give you the authority to trample on serpents (the devil) *and scorpions* (demons)*, and over all the power of the enemy, and nothing shall by any means hurt you (Luke 10:18,19)."*

Nothing is going to hurt us. The devil and demons are subject to us through the name of Jesus.

Paul instructed us, *And whatever you do in word or deed, do all in the name of the Lord Jesus (Colossians 3:17a).*

Everything we do in word or action, we are to do in the name of Jesus. From the time we get up in the morning until we go to bed at night, we are to do it in the name of Jesus. What a responsibility this puts on us.

What would happen in your day if you actually lived by these instructions?

What if Jesus got out of bed with you in the morning and as you walked through your day, you handled every circumstance as if Jesus were right there with you? Would things be different in your life?

That is God's plan for every believer. When we act as though Jesus is with us every moment, people will marvel. People will ask, "By what authority are you doing these things?"

The normal walk of the believer in doing the daily tasks of life would be a witness to the world. Through the lives of the believers, the world would know the name of Jesus.

Paul wrote, *Let this mind be in you which was also in Christ Jesus, who, being in the form of God, did not consider it robbery to be equal with God, but made Himself of no reputation, taking the form of a servant, and coming in the likeness of men.*

And being found in appearance as a man, He humbled Himself and became obedient to the point of death, even the death of the cross.

Therefore God also has highly exalted Him and given Him the name which is above every name, that at the name of Jesus every knee should bow, of those in heaven, and of those on earth, and of those under the earth, and that every tongue should confess that Jesus Christ is Lord, to the glory of God the Father (Philippians 2:5-11).

The name of Jesus is above every name. His name is above the name of any circumstance that you can come against. His name is greater than the name of a headache. His name is greater than the name of a flu. It's greater than the name of any cancer.

At the mention of the name of Jesus, blind eyes are still opening. The deaf and dumb are still hearing and speaking. The lame are walking. Those with heart disease and cancer are being healed.

It's also important we realize the authority we have when we ask God for any need in our lives in the name of Jesus. The writer of the book of Hebrews said, *Let us therefore come boldly to the throne of grace, that we may obtain mercy and find grace to help in time of need* (Hebrews 4:16).

Jesus was talking to His disciples when He said, *Most assuredly, I say to you, he who believes in Me, the*

*works that I do he will do also; and greater works than
these he will do, because I go to My Father.*

*And whatever you ask in My name, that I will do,
that the Father may be glorified in the Son.*

If you ask anything in My name, I will do it (John
14:12-14).

Often we hear people say, "Whatever we ask in
His name ...," and they claim this as God's promise to
fulfill their own desires. It's important to understand
the context and meaning of this verse. The things we
are to ask in the name of Jesus aren't to satisfy our
own selfish desires. We are to ask for those things that
will cause the Father to be glorified in the Son.

The things we are to ask in Jesus' name are
primarily those that will equip us to do the works of
Jesus. Jesus spent His time preaching, teaching, and
destroying the works of the devil. He brought hope to
the hopeless, healed the sick, and cast out demons.

Jesus said we could do these things in the
authority of His name. He promised we could have
everything we needed to do them by simply asking for
them. Jesus also said, *and greater works than these
shall he* (who believes) *do: because I go unto my Father.*

When we think of the wonderful works of Jesus,
our minds have difficulty in understanding how we
could do "greater works."

These "greater works" are possible because God
has empowered believers with the same power of the
Holy Spirit which was in Jesus. God has also restored
authority on this earth back to believers.

When Jesus ministered on this earth, a legal
struggle over authority took place. Jesus as the "last

Adam," a man without sin, could legally operate in authority as Adam had been created to do. Satan also had authority because it had been surrendered to him by Adam and Eve when they sinned.

As Jesus ministered, a great battle took place over the issue of who had the right to "authority" on this earth. It is obvious from the outcome, that the authority Jesus operated in as the "last Adam" superseded Satan's authority. As a man, Jesus operated in the original, primary authority that had been given to mankind immediately after they were created. Satan was operating in a secondary authority taken from Adam and Eve.

Today, our authority as believers is legally undeniable. It is based on the completed work of Jesus. He redeemed us by His precious blood from Satan's dominion. He delivered to the depths of the earth the sins that caused us to lose our authority. He snatched the keys of authority away from the devil when He rose triumphantly from the grave. He spoiled (disarmed, disrobed and bound) principalities and powers and put them to an open shame. He stripped them of all legal authority on this earth.

Legal authority has been restored to every believer. Believers are the ones to whom He has given "the keys to the kingdom." Since the authority of the believers is based on the completed work of Jesus, all dominion is to be done "in His name!"

There is no longer a legal contest over dominion. All Satan can do is deceive believers into thinking he has more power and authority than they do. He can try to keep believers from discovering and operating in their God-given, restored authority. He can try to bring defeat through temptation, accusation, guilt and condemnation. However, all he can do to bring defeat is what believers let him do.

Believers, with a revelation of their restored authority, can not only do "the works of Jesus," but also do even "greater works" than He did. Once again men and women have been restored to their original position of authority on this earth. Once again God is saying, "Let them have dominion!" Now believers have the authority to bind Satan and loose the captives.

Jesus said it was to their advantage that He go away. *Nevertheless I tell you the truth. It is to your advantage that I go away; for if I do not go away, the Helper will not come to you; but if I depart, I will send Him to you (John 16:7).*

When Jesus went to His Father, He totally defeated the devil and all demon powers. When He went to His Father, the Holy Spirit came to give power to the believers. Just before He left, Jesus said, *For John truly baptized with water, but you shall be baptized with the Holy Spirit not many days from now.*

But you shall receive power when the Holy Spirit has come upon you; and you shall be witnesses to Me in Jerusalem, and in all Judea and Samaria, and to the end of the earth (Acts 1:5,8).

When Jesus ascended to His Father, He made it possible for us to continue His works in an even greater way on earth. Now His works wouldn't be limited to one person, one group of people, one village, one city, or even one nation at a time. Through believers, the works He did could take place in every village, city, and nation around the world simultaneously.

The power for these works is to be manifested through the power of the Holy Spirit. The authority to do these works is in the name of Jesus. The money and provision to do these greater works are to be provided when believers ask using the name of Jesus.

Many years ago, when we were ministering in Hong Kong, we were at a special Chinese New Year's meeting at a large Christian high school.

One of the students had been suffering from a condition that caused one of her legs to swell to over twice the size of the other. She had been in the hospital, but when she heard of the meeting, she had come on crutches to ask for prayer. Her swollen leg was tightly wrapped with an elastic bandage.

As I leaned over and touched her leg, I boldly said, "Jesus, touch her."

It was as though someone had stuck a pin in an inflated balloon. There was a "swish" of sound as the elastic bandage fell loosely around her ankle. She had been instantly, and totally, healed by the power and authority of the name of Jesus.

Her crutches fell to the floor, and she began to run and shout. "I'm healed! I'm healed!"

The excitement among the students was electrifying when they saw for themselves a demonstration of the power of the name of Jesus, a power they will never forget.

Equipped with the provision, the power, and the authority of the name of Jesus, the church is to go into all the world and preach the gospel to every creature.

Every city, state and nation can be taken away from the devil when each believer begins forcefully to advance the kingdom of God at home, at work, and around the world.

Chapter Eleven

Jesus,
The Authority of His Name

For several years, I was general manager of the largest chain of Christian bookstores in the Western United States. I would often fly into a city to visit the stores and spend time training and directing the store managers and their staff.

During these visits, I would evaluate the store's operation and give directions in areas I felt needed to be changed. Time was spent in getting to know the managers and their families.

Often the managers would take me to the airport when I was preparing to leave. We would talk about many things while I was in town. However, just before I boarded the plane, I would summarize and emphasize the most important instructions I wanted to leave with them. This was never the time for idle talk.

In the last chapter of Mark, we find Jesus preparing to leave this earth. These were his final moments with His disciples and He gave them His final instructions. What important words did He leave ringing in their ears?

And He said to them, "Go into all the world and preach the gospel to every creature. He who believes and is baptized will be saved; but he who does not believe will be condemned (Mark 16:15,16)."

Many Christians are so comfortable with their beautiful churches and extensive church programs that they seem to have forgotten these last important words of Jesus. They have lost their vision to reach the world with the gospel.

I have been in many places of the world where people are living in total bondage to empty religions, sin, demon worship, sickness, poverty and death. They have never heard the name of Jesus. They are crying out in hopeless despair. "Is there no one who cares?"

Has the church forgotten its primary responsibility? Has the church lost its understanding of power and authority and become discouraged and given up the task?

Jesus continued with these important words, *And these signs will follow those who believe: In My name they will cast out demons; they will speak with new tongues; they will take up serpents* (the devil); *and if they drink anything deadly, it will by no means hurt them; they will lay hands on the sick, and they will recover (Mark 16:17,18).*

For years we waited for these signs to be in our lives and ministry so we would feel prepared to go. But Mark wrote that these signs would follow, not precede. First, the body of Christ, the church, must obey God and go into all the world and preach the gospel, then the signs will follow. They cannot follow us if we aren't going anywhere and if we aren't preaching the gospel.

Today, many students, working men and women, and homemakers are realizing that this command is for all believers. They are realizing these signs aren't just for ministers or missionaries. These signs are for all those who believe. Today, believers are walking in faith in their homes, neighborhoods, schools or businesses, and miracles are following them. They are taking their vacations to places where they can tell people about Jesus, and when they go, signs are following.

When the translators were trying to clarify this passage, they added punctuation after "those who believe." This passage could just as correctly read "those who believe in my name." Many believers don't know the power of believing in the name of Jesus. When we believe in His name, we will use His name in the power of the Holy Spirit and signs will follow.

The first sign that will follow the preaching of the gospel is casting out devils. This was a normal, everyday part of the ministry of Jesus. Today, many people are being bothered by demon spirits even as they were in the day of Jesus. Casting out devils does not require someone with a "special ministry." This sign is for everyone who believes in the name of Jesus.

Jesus said, *In My name they* (believers)*will cast out demons.* Notice, we don't ask them to come out. We don't beg them to come out. We cast, or drive, them out by using the name of Jesus.

Stan was seventeen years old when he came to me for help when I was administrative assistant to the pastor of one of the largest churches in California. Stan's father was a highly respected Christian doctor who owned a clinic in his home town in the Midwestern part of the United States. Sometime before, Stan had left home in rebellion.

From rebellion, he had gone into drugs, illicit sex and perversion. He had learned that by inviting spirits to come into his body, he could control people, and he often used this power on teen-age girls to satisfy his own lustful desires.

For more power, Stan invited more demons to come in, until one day, he realized he was no longer in control. The demons were controlling him.

When I first met him, he was in absolute, total bondage to those demon powers. The voice that came from this teen-ager was the deep, gravely voice of an old man. He was tormented and in despair.

After he told me his story, I looked at him and the Spirit of God gave me wisdom. I knew Stan wanted to get rid of the demons that were controlling him, but still wanted to keep the demons that gave him the power to control others. I had to get his attention. There was only one answer to his problem. I pushed back from my desk, stood up and I said, "Stan, I'm sorry. I just can't help you."

He sat in stunned silence, and the color seemed to drain from his face.

After a long pause, I continued, "Unless you are ready to commit your life one hundred percent to Jesus as Lord of your life."

He sat there and stared at me for several minutes. He knew he had no choice. Finally, he sighed and answered, "All right!" and I sat back down.

Stan began to confess his sins to God, and as he did, he received forgiveness and cleansing. He renounced his rebellion against his parents and his involvement with drugs, illicit sex, the occult and the demon spirits he had invited into his body.

I said, "Satan, I bind you in the name of Jesus!" Then I commanded the demon spirits to come out in the name of Jesus. They began to scream and Stan began to shake and throw his arms violently. I commanded the demons to quit manifesting themselves, to be quiet, and come out in Jesus' name. I began to quote the Word of God to the demon spirits.

And they overcame him (Satan) *by the blood of the Lamb and by the word of their testimony (Revelation 12:11a).*

Behold, I give you the authority to trample on serpents and scorpions, and over all the power of the enemy, and nothing shall by any means hurt you (Luke 10:19).

And these signs will follow those who believe: In My name they will cast out demons (Mark 16:17a).

But if I cast out demons by the Spirit of God, surely the kingdom of God has come upon you. Or else how can one enter a strong man's house and plunder his goods, unless he first binds the strong man? And then he will plunder his house (Matthew 12:28,29).

You are of God, little children, and have overcome them, because He who is in you is greater than he who is in the world (1 John 4:4).

Therefore submit to God. Resist the devil and he will flee from you (James 4:7).

Stan and I were protected by the blood of Jesus. I overcame Satan and his demons by the Word of God, and in the name of Jesus, I commanded the demon spirits to leave.

One by one, as the Lord led me, I commanded the tormenting spirits, the spirits of rebellion, drug abuse and the occult to come out. I continued with authority. "You controlling spirits come out! You spirits of lust and perversion, come out in the name of Jesus."

In just a few minutes time, Stan was completely delivered.

The first words that came out of his mouth were completely normal. He sounded like a seventeen year old boy again. The tormenting spirits were gone. He began to grow in his Christian life as he spent time in the Word, fellowshipping with other Christians, and coming to church. His life was completely changed. Stan called his parents, who had been praying for him. They flew to California and he was reunited with his family.

Jesus mentioned a number of signs that would follow those who believe in His name. He ended the list with these important words, *They will lay hands on the sick, and they will recover.* The last words Jesus spoke on this earth revealed His continued compassion for the sick. For three and a half years, everywhere Jesus went, He healed the sick. He healed those who were oppressed of the devil.

Mark tells us about these final moments. *So then, after the Lord had spoken to them, He was received up into heaven, and sat down at the right hand of God.*

And they went out and preached everywhere, the Lord working with them and confirming the word through the accompanying signs. Amen (Mark 16:19,20).

In obedience, the disciples preached the gospel, and the Lord worked with them and through them by the power of the Holy Spirit. Exactly as Jesus had promised, "the signs followed."

What was the purpose of the signs? Were they to draw a crowd and to entertain? Were they an endorsement of the life and ministry of the disciples? What was the purpose of the supernatural signs that were to follow every believer? Jesus said they were for the purpose of "confirming the Word."

On one of my trips to India, the Lord led me, with a team of men, to go to a beach area on the west coast of South India. The sun was setting as we arrived and set up an amplifier and a light under the beautiful palm trees at the edge of the beach. There were no churches in this strong Hindu area, and only a very small percentage of the people had ever heard about Jesus.

The communist flags were flying. The hammer and sickle, symbols of the communist party, could be seen painted on walls and fences and even embedded with tiles in the pavement of the street. The people had heard the lies and empty promises of these godless atheists who had exploited them. They had heard about Lenin and Stalin and other communist leaders, but they had never heard about Jesus and His love.

As some of our team began to sing, the children came to listen. Soon hundreds gathered as one member of the team began to tell Bible stories. Next the adults began to come. Soon, as far as I could see into the darkness of the night, a sea of brown faces were looking back at us. Hundreds had gathered and were sitting on the sand under the palm trees.

I began to pray. "Lord, what can I preach to them that they will understand?" I could exclaim, "The Bible says ..."

"But what's the Bible?" they would ask.

I could answer, "It's the Word of God."

"But which god?" they would reply. The Hindus had thousands of gods.

When I stood to preach, I very simply told them the gospel. I told them that Jesus was the Son of God and that He loved them and had even died for them. I told them how they could receive eternal life by accepting His forgiveness and receiving Jesus as their personal Savior.

I knew this was the first time many of them had heard of Jesus, the Son of God. Why should they believe me? I knew God had promised that if believers would go and preach, He would confirm His Word with signs following. I expected God to heal a number of them to confirm that what I had taught them was true.

I knew God was speaking through me. Suddenly, I heard myself boldly state that God was going to demonstrate to them that this was His Word and that I had told them the truth. As I continued, speaking with boldness and authority, I heard myself announce, "God is going to heal all of you." My natural mind cringed, "Oh, no, Lord, you must mean some of them." I knew, however, it was God speaking through me by His Holy Spirit.

The team stood with me and we began to lay our hands on the sick. The team included several believers who had been called into ministry, but it also included a salesman and an auto mechanic. We were ordinary believers who had obeyed God and had "gone forth" as Jesus had commanded. When we laid our hands on their sick bodies, we simply said, "Be healed in the name of Jesus!"

Many were healed of asthma, back problems, and pain in their bodies. One young man who had been born deaf and dumb was instantly healed, and at our instruction was saying, "Praise the Lord, Praise the Lord" in his native language. By the hundreds, they kept coming for prayer and just as God had said, there wasn't one person we ministered to who wasn't instantly healed. God confirmed His Word. He healed them all.

When everyone who wanted to be prayed for had been healed by the power of God, I carefully explained to the crowd that it was the power of Jesus that had healed them. I quickly repeated the gospel message. Again, I told them who Jesus was. I made it clear there was just one God and that Jesus was His only Son.

I knew they had thousands of demon idols and I knew they would be willing to accept Jesus as just one more god. So I made it clear that Jesus said that He was the only way, that no one could come into a relationship with the Father-God except through Him. I told them that to receive Jesus as their Savior, they would have to renounce and destroy all their idols and and accept Jesus as the only way of salvation.

I then asked anyone who would like to invite Jesus to come into his or her heart, to stand up. I thought there might be a few who would make that decision. To my amazement, they all stood up. I thought, "They must have misunderstood me. Perhaps the young man interpreting hasn't made it clear." I had them all sit down.

Again I presented the gospel as clearly as I could. I made certain they understood the full implications of their decision. Their whole lives centered around the Hindu religion and idol worship. Again I asked, "Now is there anyone who will forsake all other gods and invite Jesus Christ to come into your life." They all stood up.

Again, I thought they had misunderstood me. I had them sit down and I presented the gospel the third time. I made it harder. I made sure they knew that to make this commitment, they would have to renounce all their idols and that they could never go back to the Hindu temple.

I asked those who would make the decision to follow Jesus and Him alone as their only Lord and Savior to stand up. Once again, they all stood up! As they prayed the sinner's prayer with me, in a few moment's time, the people of that whole village passed out of the kingdom of darkness into the kingdom of God's dear Son.

We had gone to the uttermost part of the world. We had gone in obedience to Jesus' command and had preached the gospel. We had obeyed God and laid our hands on the sick. We had believed in the authority and power of the name of Jesus. God had confirmed His Word to these precious people by healing signs and wonders. As a result, we had experienced the same powerful results as the disciples in the early days of the church.

Immediately after Jesus had given His last important words of instruction to His believers, *He was received up into heaven, and sat down at the right hand of God (Mark 16:19b).* The book of Acts tells us, *Now when He had spoken these things, while they watched, He was taken up, and a cloud received Him out of their sight (Acts 1:9).*

Jesus was gone, but His works were to continue. His body on earth is now made up of every believer. We are now His legs and His feet. We are now His arms and His hands. We are His body. We are to be called the church, and the gates of hell cannot prevail against us.

When Jesus first mentioned the church to His disciples, He said the gates of Hades couldn't prevail against it. He instructed the disciples that they were to minister in His name. He also told them to wait for the power of the Holy Spirit to come upon them.

On the day of Pentecost, the church received the power of the Holy Spirit. Peter, who less than two months before had weakly denied Jesus, was now standing boldly, preaching the gospel of Jesus with powerful results.

Then fear came upon every soul, and many wonders and signs were done through the apostles.

And the Lord added to the church daily those who were being saved (Acts 2:43,47b).

The book of Acts is the story of these things coming into existence. It's the history of the very beginnings of the church and it's a history book unparalleled in reading and excitement!

The power of the Holy Spirit came, and when the people heard and saw the marvelous things that were happening, about three thousand people became believers in Jesus Christ in one day.

We are taken immediately from that exciting beginning to an account of two of the disciples, Peter and John, as they were walking to the temple *(Acts 3:1-16)*. They saw a beggar laying beside the gate of the temple. We know they had passed him before because the Bible says that he had been born crippled and he was carried to the temple gate daily. As usual, the beggar asked Peter and John for money, but this time Peter looked right at him and demanded, *Look at us!*

Then Peter said, "Silver and gold I do not have, but what I do have I give you: In the name of Jesus Christ of Nazareth, rise up and walk."

Peter and John didn't have money that day, but what they did have was much more valuable. They had the name of Jesus! And they knew the authority and power that was released in His name.

Peter reached out to the beggar and taking him by his right hand, lifted him up. Immediately, his feet and ankles became strong. *So he, leaping up, stood and walked and entered the temple with them—walking, leaping, and praising God.* He couldn't contain his excitement.

The people in the temple knew the beggar. They had passed him week after week and year after year. They were amazed to see him walking and leaping. Immediately, a crowd gathered.

This is the first story we have of individuals walking in the power and authority of the name of Jesus after Jesus left this earth.

Peter began to teach. He said, *Men of Israel, why do you marvel at this? Or why look so intently at us, as though by our own power or godliness we had made this man walk?* He told them it was Jesus who was being glorified. *And His name, through faith in His name, has made this man strong.*

An even larger crowd gathered, and Peter preached to them. He told them about Jesus. Over five thousand believed and accepted Jesus as their Savior from this one gathering, the result of one wonderful miracle.

The religious leaders in the temple were not happy about this healing or the meeting following. They were so upset they held the two disciples until they could call a hearing the following day *(Acts 4:7-30)*.

At the hearing, the first question the religious leaders asked was, *By what power or by what name have you done this?*

Peter was ready. *Filled with the Holy Spirit,* [he] *said to them "Rulers of the people and elders of Israel:*

"If we this day are judged for a good deed done to the helpless man, by what means he has been made well, let it be known to you all, and to all the people of Israel, that by the name of Jesus Christ of Nazareth,

*whom you crucified, whom God raised from the dead,
by Him this man stands here before you whole.*

*Nor is there salvation in any other, for there is no
other name under heaven given among men by which
we must be saved.*

What could the religious leaders say? They saw
the boldness of Peter and John, and they knew they
had been disciples of Jesus. They could see the beggar
standing there completely healed. There had been a
great miracle. They couldn't deny it.

The religious leaders wanted to punish the disciples, but they couldn't. *For, indeed, that a notable
miracle has been done through them is evident to all
who dwell in Jerusalem, and we cannot deny it.*

Instead, they compromised. *But so that it
spreads no further among the people, let us severely
threaten them, that from now on they speak to no man
in this name. And they called them and commanded
them not to speak at all nor teach in the name of Jesus.*
They knew the source of Peter and John's authority
and power. They knew it was the name of Jesus.

Peter and John wouldn't compromise. They became even more bold and they prayed with the other
believers, *Now, Lord, look on their threats, and grant
to Your servants that with all boldness they may speak
Your word, by stretching out Your hand to heal, and
that signs and wonders may be done through the name
of Your holy Servant Jesus.*

The believers of the early church had discovered
for themselves that the words of Jesus were true.
When they preached in the name of Jesus, God did
confirm His Word with supernatural signs and

miracles. As a result, many were responding to the message of salvation and were becoming a part of the body of Christ.

And through the hands of the apostles many signs and wonders were done among the people. And they were all with one accord in Solomon's Porch.

And believers were increasingly added to the Lord, multitudes of both men and women.

Also a multitude gathered from the surrounding cities to Jerusalem, bringing sick people and those who were tormented by unclean spirits, and they were all healed.

Again the religious leaders were filled with indignation and had the disciples thrown into prison. This time an angel opened the prison doors, and told them to *Go, stand in the temple and speak to the people all the words of this life (Acts 5:12-40).* This is God's message to believers, even today. We are to go, to stand and to speak.

We are to go to our "Jerusalem, Judea, and Samaria." We are to begin in our homes, neighborhoods, offices and schools. We are to go to our cities, states, and nations. We are to go the uttermost parts of the world. When we go, we are to stand in the authority of the name of Jesus.

When we go and stand, we are also to speak. As with Peter and John, we are to speak and tell Jesus' words of life. And when we obey, God will confirm His Word and like in the book of Acts, the Lord will add to the church daily such as should be saved.

Again the religious leaders held a hearing for the apostles *saying, "Did we not strictly command you not to teach in this name? And look, you have filled Jerusalem with your doctrine!" Again, Peter and the other apostles answered and taught them about Jesus.*

This time, the religious leaders wanted to kill them, but still fearing the people, they beat them instead. Again they commanded them that they shouldn't speak in the name of Jesus.

Even today, those who have been deceived by Satan's counterfeit religions are saying, "It's all right to teach and preach anything you want, just don't mention the name of Jesus!"

The believers of the early days of the church obeyed Jesus. They used the authority of His name, and the whole world was shaken and great numbers were saved. The authority of the name of Jesus wasn't just for the apostles. As Jesus said, it's for all those who believe.

We wonder why the church is weak today; why we see so few miracles; why so few are being saved. Could it be that the church has forgotten the command of Jesus to go to all the world and in His name to cast out devils and heal the sick?

Could it be that as God is restoring the truth of our authority and dominion to the church, the church of our day will be as the church of the book of Acts? A church that the gates of hell will not be able to prevail against.

Philip was a layman in the early days of the church. He was known for his honesty and integrity, and he was full of the Holy Spirit. We are first told of him when he was among those chosen to serve as deacons to help take care of some routine functions of the church *(Acts 6:1-6)*.

The Apostles had been preaching the gospel in Jerusalem and Judea, but Philip remembered the command of Jesus, that they were also to be witnesses in Samaria and to the end of the earth.

Samaria wasn't a favorite place for a Jew to go. They hated the Samaritans. However, prejudice no longer had place in Philip's life. He, a layman, simply obeyed the command of Jesus. We are told that Philip went to the city of Samaria, and preached about Christ, *and the multitudes with one accord heeded the things spoken by Philip, hearing and seeing the miracles which he did.*

Why should they believe Philip? Why should these Samaritans listen and give heed to a despised Jew? Because they were hearing and seeing the miracles that he did. *For unclean spirits, crying with a loud voice, came out of many who were possessed; and many who were paralyzed and lame were healed.*

And there was great joy in that city.

But when they believed Philip as he preached the things concerning the kingdom of God and the name of Jesus Christ, both men and women were baptized (Acts 8:4-8,12).

Philip was an ordinary layman who obeyed God and preached in the name of Jesus. God confirmed His Word with great signs, wonders and miracles, and as a result, a great revival came to that city.

For too long, the church has thought itself too sophisticated for signs and miracles. However, the world is hungry for the supernatural and thousands are turning to the occult. Today more than ever, we need supernatural miracles to demonstrate that God's message of salvation through Jesus Christ is true.

As the church is regaining the knowledge of the authority and power of the name of Jesus, signs and wonders are following and confirming the preaching of God's Word. With the authority of the name of Jesus restored to the church, in the days ahead as in the book of Acts, we are going to see greater and greater numbers responding to the gospel.

Saul, a religious leader, was persecuting the disciples of the Lord. You know the story recorded in the book of Acts. A light appeared to Saul and he met Jesus on the road to Damascus. Then, the Lord appeared to Ananias in a vision, and told him to go to Saul, and to lay hands on him, but Ananias answered, *And here he has authority from the chief priests to bind all who call on Your name.* Ananias needed more reassurance. The Lord told Ananias that Saul was a *chosen vessel of Mine to bear My name before Gentiles, kings, and the children of Israel. For I will show him how many things he must suffer for My name's sake (Acts 9:10-16).*

Saul became the great missionary, Paul, who was chosen by God to be His witness to the uttermost part of the earth. Paul had been chosen to bear a name. It wasn't to be the name of a religion; it wasn't to be the name of a denomination; it was to be the name of Jesus. With that name, Paul shook the nations of the world.

When Paul arrived at Ephesus, he spent three months teaching in the synagogue and two years teaching in a Bible school, *And this continued for two years, so that all who dwelt in Asia heard the word of the Lord Jesus, both Jews and Greeks. Now God worked unusual miracles by the hands of Paul, so that even handkerchiefs or aprons were brought from his body to the sick, and the diseases left them and the evil spirits went out of them.* We also read that *fear fell on them all, and the name of the Lord Jesus was magnified (Acts 19:8-12,17).*

All Asia Minor was reached with the gospel because the name of Jesus was magnified.

Today there is arising an army of men and women who aren't ashamed to bear the name of Jesus. When they go with the authority of that name, the Word of God grows mightily and the gates of hell cannot prevail against them. They are the church triumphant. They know the authority and power of the name of Jesus.

Chapter Twelve

The Church Triumphant

Fanned by brisk, dry summer winds, the fire was roaring down the hillside in Southern California. Hundreds of firefighters were desperately trying to head off this raging inferno of destruction. A Christian ranch for emotionally disturbed children was located directly in its path. At that time, Joyce and I were closely involved with this ministry.

Joyce had gone into the dry cleaners in a nearby shopping center. When she came out, she saw the fire on the hillside threatening this ranch and the homes in the canyon. Joyce, knowing her God-given authority and dominion, stopped in the middle of the parking lot. She forgot the people that might be around. She pushed her dry cleaning, purse and car keys into one hand and pointed at the fire on the hillside above with the other. Acting in bold confidence, she took authority over the fire. She said, "Fire, I command you, in the name of Jesus, to stop burning!"

The local newspaper reported the next morning, "Fire in Anaheim Hills suddenly and mysteriously stops burning."

As Joyce was going about doing the normal activities of life, in a moment of extreme danger, she had used her God-given authority to avoid a tragedy.

Another time, we were ministering with Charles and Frances Hunter in meetings in San Diego. After the evening meeting, we were in their hotel room talking excitedly about the miracles we had just seen.

It had been raining heavily and several mud slides had destroyed homes in the area that week. The late news was on television, and Joyce heard the words, "New rain storms are headed toward San Diego."

She tried to get the attention of the rest of us in the room, but we were so busy talking about the wonderful presence of God in the previous meeting that we didn't hear her. She said, "San Diego is in danger from another storm. We need to pray." She tried two more times to get our attention.

Suddenly, Joyce pointed her hand in the direction of the storm. When we heard the authority in her voice, she had our attention and our agreement. "In the name of Jesus, storm, I command you to turn around and go another way. You can't touch this area!"

The next morning the headlines of the San Diego paper said, "Rainstorm veers suddenly to the north and misses San Diego."

Several years later when we were living in Texas, a Mexican oil well erupted in the Gulf of Mexico and a huge oil slick was heading toward the Texas beaches. Every day the newspapers ran feature stories about the destruction that was coming to the fish and wildlife along the coast. The resort hotels and beach areas would be devastated. Millions of dollars would be lost by our fishing and tourist industries. We read and heard about the bad news for days.

The Governor of the State of Texas had flown over the miles of blackened sea that was destined to reach our beaches the following week, and he declared hundreds of miles of our Texas beaches a disaster area.

I was teaching the Adult Bible Class in the auditorium of Lakewood Church in Houston the following Sunday morning when faith rose within me to take authority and dominion over that oil slick.

Why should we as Christians let this happen to our beaches? Hadn't God given us dominion over the earth? Were we not to subdue and have dominion over everything on this earth?

I talked to the class about the oil slick and about our authority as believers. I asked everyone who would agree with me in faith to stand. The whole class stood, turned around and pointed in the direction of the Gulf of Mexico.

I began to speak to the oil slick. I boldly declared, "No! Oil slick, you aren't going to do this to our beaches! In the name of Jesus, I command you to stop!" I paused for a moment searching in my spirit for the right words to continue. "I command you to dissipate and go back out to sea!"

Again, we read the results of our prayers in the headlines of the newspapers that week. First the articles reported the oil slick had seemed to lose direction. Within a few days, a news reporter used the exact words the Lord had given me to say. "Mexican oil slick unexpectedly 'dissipates'," he wrote. He continued to say the oil slick was for some unexplained reason breaking up and going back out to sea.

The first thing that God said about Adam and Eve when He created them was, "Let them have dominion." Men and women were created to rule over this earth. After Satan's deception, they lost this dominion. The Son of God endured the agony of the cross. Then He fought and won the greatest battle of all eternity to restore dominion to men and women!

God didn't lead Joyce and me to pray and ask Him to stop the fire, the storm, or the oil slick. We didn't pray, "Please, God, if it be your will, stop this destruction."

God created people to walk in absolute authority and dominion on this earth. He said, *Behold, I give you the authority to trample on serpents and scorpions, and over all the power of the enemy, and nothing shall by any means hurt you (Luke 10:19)*. God didn't reserve any authority on this earth for Himself. He said it had all been given to His new creation. For God to come to this earth and exercise authority and dominion now, He would need to take that authority away from his people.

Jesus could change water into wine, feed the five thousand, curse the fig tree, calm the sea, heal the sick, cast out devils, and raise the dead. He walked in authority when He was living on this earth.

You may be thinking, "He was the Son of God, of course, He could do anything because He was God."

John quoted some interesting words that Jesus said, *The dead will hear the voice of the Son of God; and those who hear will live. For as the Father has life in Himself, so He has granted the Son to have life in Himself, and has given Him authority to execute judgment also, because He is the Son of Man (John 5:25-27).*

As the Son of God, Jesus could impart eternal life to the spiritually dead. But notice, it says the Father had given Him "authority," not because He was the "Son of God," but because he was the "Son of man."

When Jesus walked in authority and dominion on this earth, when he calmed the sea, healed the sick, and cast out devils, He didn't do it as the Son of God. He did it as the Son of man. For it was men and women, not God, who were to walk with authority and dominion over this earth and everything that is in it.

If Jesus had exercised authority as the Son of God on the earth, He would have been violating His plan and purpose for mankind to walk in authority and dominion on this earth.

Many people still think of themselves as poor, weak Christians, whose only hope in this life is the intervention of God on their behalf. Not realizing who they are, or the power they have, they keep begging God to help them.

"Please, God," they pray, "stop all these terrible things the devil is trying to do to me!" They don't realize that God has already given them everything they need to win.

When we begin to realize who we are in Jesus Christ, when we begin to understand that we have been created in the image of God, just a little lower than God, to walk as God with absolute authority and dominion over this earth, it will revolutionize our lives. We will no longer be losers, we will be winners.

Men and women were not made for defeat! They were created to walk every day of their lives in total victory. Paul wrote, *But thanks be to God, who gives us the victory through our Lord Jesus Christ (1 Corinthians 15:57).*

Yes, the human race is at war, but now we can know who the real enemy is. We can know what our spiritual weapons are, and that these weapons are mighty through God to the pulling down of strongholds. We can walk in victory.

As God is restoring this truth to the body of Christ today, He wants us to take this world away from the devil. To do this, we must begin where we live. We are to walk in authority and dominion in our homes, neighborhoods, schools and offices. When we do this, we will be preparing ourselves for even greater victories.

God's lessons on authority often begin with the small testings in our lives. Several years ago, we had a gas dryer, and the automatic gas valve would often fail to open. Joyce would ask me to get the dryer started several times a month. I would take the bottom panel off the dryer and tap on the valve until the dryer began to work. This became a frequent source of frustration to both of us.

One day, I walked into the laundry room and laying my hands on the dryer, exclaimed, "I command you, work in the name of Jesus." Instantly, I heard the valve open and the gas rushing into the burner. Soon, every time Joyce asked me to make the dryer work, I would lay my hands on it and say, "In the name of Jesus, work!" and the valve would instantly open.

This had been occurring for many weeks and had become a part of the routine of our home. One evening, I was sitting in the family room talking to a friend who was a dean at a large university. We were very involved with our conversation when Joyce called out, "A.L., the dryer isn't working."

Without stopping the conversation, I got up and walked toward the laundry room. My friend followed me. My thoughts were still on our conversation. When we walked into the laundry room, I stopped our conversation just long enough to say, "In the name of Jesus, start!" As usual, the dryer started and I turned to walk out of the room.

As I resumed the conversation, I realized my friend was no longer with me, and I turned around to see him still standing beside the dryer, staring at it in amazement. "A.L., is that a usual occurrence around here?" he hesitantly asked.

People have failed for so long to walk in their God-given authority that what should be normal Christian behavior, seems abnormal. The more Christians walk in their authority and dominion on this earth the more the supernatural will appear to be the expected, normal routine of life.

We shouldn't always deal with our worn out appliances in this manner. We should have been believing God for a new dryer! However, God did use this simple example to teach us more about authority.

Jesus didn't go around turning water into wine, or walking on water as a parlor trick to amuse His friends. Jesus said, *Most assuredly, I say to you, the Son can do nothing of Himself, but what He sees the*

Father do; for whatever He does, the Son also does in like manner (John 5:19).

To walk in authority, our daily walk with our heavenly Father must be such that we aren't led by our own desires, but rather by what we see the Father doing. When we know how to walk in authority, our faith and the faith of others will no longer be hindered. We will learn to walk in obedience, to grow in faith and to experience great signs and wonders in our daily lives.

We are at war. We have an enemy who has come to steal from us, and if possible, to destroy us. Peter warned us, *Be sober, be vigilant; because your adversary the devil walks about like a roaring lion, seeking whom he may devour.*

Resist him, steadfast in the faith (1 Peter 5:8,9a).

If we don't know and use our spiritual authority, he can devour us. He can steal from us and even destroy us. I am persuaded we aren't going to let this happen because we now know who we are in Jesus Christ. We know who the real enemy is. We know our real battle is with a foe who has already been defeated. We know our real warfare isn't with *flesh and blood, but against principalities, against powers, against the rulers of the darkness of this age, against spiritual hosts of wickedness in the heavenly places (Ephesians 6:12).*

Yet in all these things we are more than conquerors through Him who loved us. For I am persuaded that neither death nor life, nor angels nor principalities nor powers, nor things present nor things to come, nor height nor depth, nor any other created thing, shall be able to separate us from the love of God which is in Christ Jesus our Lord (Romans 8:37-39).

Many years ago, we listened to a cassette tape, "The Power of the Name of Jesus." The following weekend I was driving down the highway late at night. Joyce was beside me in the front seat. She was almost asleep, but her mind was drifting back over the teaching we had just received on the power of the name of Jesus.

I was directly behind another car traveling at highway speed. Suddenly, I saw a police car with flashing red lights speeding into the intersection immediately ahead of us. The police car was on a direct collision course with the car in front of me. At the speed we were all traveling, it seemed impossible to avoid a terrible crash. I knew I couldn't stop in time, and our car would pile into the others.

As I slammed on the brakes, I saw something very strange happen on the highway ahead of us. The police car was suddenly turned parallel to — going the same direction as the car ahead. The patrol car hadn't swerved, there was no squealing of tires, there had been no time to turn. It was, in an instant, going in another direction traveling at the same speed on the shoulder of the road next to the car ahead. I could hardly believe my eyes.

That is what I saw. What had really happened was in the spirit realm. Joyce had opened her eyes just in time to see the police car coming into the intersection. She had reacted instantly by pointing at the police car and shouting, "Jesus!"

When she saw the approaching danger, she was alert, she was sober and vigilant, and the adversary had failed again in his plans to kill and devour us.

One day our daughter Kathy was involved in an accident that had done considerable damage to one of our cars. The accident hadn't been her fault, but she kept going over the details with us and asking what she could have done to have avoided it. Finally, Joyce answered, "Kathy, I really feel you did one thing wrong. I believe that if you had spoken the name of Jesus in faith, the accident could have been avoided."

Several months later, Kathy was stopped at a traffic light. Suddenly a car traveling at a high rate of speed was careening right toward her. This time she remembered the authority of Jesus' name. She pointed at the car racing straight at her and shouted, "Jesus!" She knew *The name of the Lord is a strong tower; The righteous run to it and are safe (Proverbs 18:10).*

Instantly, the approaching car hit a concrete divider in the intersection and shot into the air. It flew over the top of Kathy's car hood and struck a utility pole at the side of the road and crashed to the ground inches from her car.

As Kathy climbed from her car, she heard people shouting at her in disbelief, "Did you see that? I can't believe it! That car just flew into the air and missed your car!"

Kathy had experienced her spiritual authority and dominion. She had been alert, and Satan's plans for her life had failed. Kathy had proved the words of the prophet Joel when he said, *And it shall come to*

182

pass that whoever calls on the name of the Lord shall be saved (Joel 2:32). ———

The devil walks around like a roaring lion, seeking whom he may devour. However, when we know our spiritual authority, we don't have to be afraid. All that Satan or his demons can do is to try to scare us. We can resist him steadfastly in the faith. We are covered with the blood of Jesus. We know the power of speaking the Word of God, and we have the authority of the name of Jesus. Satan's a defeated foe.

When we begin to know the authority God has given us, when we begin to walk in victory in our personal lives, God will be able to use us to change the world. We can live in authority, and we can forcefully advance the kingdom of God.

Many years ago, Joyce and I were in a small town in Northern Canada. We prayed with the pastor's family and God led us to go into spiritual battle over the town. God led us to deal with the "ruler of the darkness."

As we prayed, we bound the devil. We began to take authority over the strongholds that controlled that area of the country. We asked the Lord to reveal the name of the strong man. Joyce prayed aloud, "Lord, if you would remove this mist, this white cloud over the town, I could see what you are trying to show me."

The pastor said, "That's strange! Almost every evangelist who comes to this area says there's a white haze over the city, and there's a terrible bondage here. It's almost as if no one can be saved."

I felt the nudging of the Holy Spirit. "White Cloud... Who was White Cloud?" I asked excitedly.

Thinking for an instant, the pastor replied, "Many years ago, White Cloud was the Indian chief of the tribe of Indians on the other side of the lake." He went on to explain that the east side of the lake had been the major Indian settlement for many years. However, when the railroad was put on the west side of the lake, a new town became the major town in that area. This had made the Indians very angry.

When I prayed, God began to give me a vision. In the spirit, I saw the Indians doing a war dance. I next saw them making a fetish of some sort to put a curse on the new town. I saw the chief lead the tribe out to the bridge crossing the lake and fasten this fetish underneath the bridge where it wouldn't be discovered.

The white cloud, or haze, that so many had seen in the spirit was the curse which had been placed there by Chief White Cloud many years before.

We dealt with it in the spirit. We broke the curse placed over the city, and we felt freedom in our spirits. We knew the battle had been won.

Within a few minutes, a knock came on the door. Some people had come to the pastor's house "because they wanted to get saved." Many people who the pastor and his wife had been praying for and witnessing to over a period of years began to come and accept Jesus as their personal Savior that day.

I talked to the pastor several weeks later and he said as Joshua did on the seventh day at Jericho, *Shout, for the Lord has given you the city (Joshua 6:16b)!*

Jesus said, *And from the days of John the Baptist until now the kingdom of heaven suffers violence, and the violent take it by force (Matthew 11:12).*

Everywhere we look, we can see that "the kingdom of heaven" has suffered violence from the forces of Satan. Satan has set up "strongholds" over city after city.

However, as the Church of Jesus Christ is receiving a fresh revelation of their God-given authority and dominion, they are becoming violent in spiritual warfare. With their new-found authority in the name of Jesus, believers are boldly pulling down strongholds and forcefully taking their cities away from the devil. They are forcefully advancing the kingdom of God around the world.

On my first trip to the nation of Malaysia, God led me to a city which had been a stronghold of the devil for many years. Several years before that time, God had led a young pastor and his wife to move to that city to start a church. Everyone said it was impossible.

This city was a stronghold of crime, drunkenness, Hinduism, Buddhism and spiritualism. Hundreds of people crowded to the Hindu and the Buddhist temples in that city because of the supernatural demonic manifestations that frequently occurred as they worshipped idols. A strong witch doctor had complete control of the town.

The pastor knew God had sent him there, and he wouldn't give up although his ministry seemed to bear very little fruit. One day, he read some books that revolutionized his life. He discovered his spiritual authority, and He set out to take his town away from the devil. He began to bind the rulers of the darkness over his city. He began to teach his church how to walk in spiritual victory.

The witch doctor who controlled that town was feared by everyone. As a boy, he had been raised in a well-to-do Indian family in the south of Malaysia. He had an overwhelming desire for great power. When he was twelve years old, he smashed his family's Hindu god because he refused to serve a god who couldn't give him the power that he desired to have.

He became involved in karate and martial arts. He knew these "arts" were often the manifestations of demon powers who entered the bodies of those who practiced them. Soon, he joined a street gang and at the age of twenty-one was the leader of the most dreaded street gang in this large city.

His quest for power continued as he studied under several "masters" of Hinduism, Buddhism and spiritualism. It took him to the strongholds of spiritualism and the occult in Thailand and Indonesia. In Indonesia, he was promised that great power would be given to him by the devil if he sat for ninety days without moving in a large jar of water into which limes had been squeezed.

His desire for power was so great, he sat in this jar for ninety days in a dark cave. His "master" gave him a mouthful of rice and some water twice a day. At the end of the ninety days, the devil appeared to him.

When the devil came to him, he gave him a golden knife and the power to make it fly through the air. He also gave him a black suit and when he put that suit on, he could "fly" through the air, levitated by demon spirits. He could "fly" to the top of a large tree. He could stand on the end of the large tropical leaves and the demons would hold his weight without the leaves bending. While wearing the black suit, he could move through the air from tree to tree.

Such was the power of the witch doctor who controlled that city. All the people were afraid of him and his fearful powers.

On many occasions, he would go into a trance. With a nineteen foot bamboo pole driven through his jaws and tongue, he would lead a procession of hundreds of people through the streets as thousands watched in awesome fear. When they took the pole out, there were no wounds.

Many people gave him money to use his witchcraft on their behalf. He controlled the organized crime. He owned the houses of prostitution. He had undisputed power over that whole area.

One day he tried to put a curse on a beautiful young lady from the church as she walked down the street. This was his method of obtaining prostitutes. But his curse didn't work! The witch doctor discovered the existence of a greater power! Searching for this ultimate power, he came to talk with the pastor, and that day he accepted Jesus as his Savior. Through deliverance, he was completely set free of every demon power. Immediately, the knife and black suit disappeared.

As a result, the former witch doctor changed his name to Elisha because he wanted a double portion of God's blessing.

When I met Elisha, he was only a year old in the Lord. Because he had known the power of Satan and his kingdom, he knew how much greater his power was in Jesus. He and the pastor, with the people in the church, actively took their city away from the devil.

In just one year, the Buddhist temple was closed because the priests had lost their power. The Hindu temple was closed and torn down. When their evil control was broken by the Spirit of God, the people lost interest in their religions. The spirit of witchcraft has been broken over the city. Five out of the eight bars in town where crime and drunkenness had prevailed were closed. A new prosperity came to the city and the church grew rapidly.

Through faith, the believers had subdued a kingdom of Satan. They turned to flight the armies of the aliens. They boldly acted as God had created them to act when He said, "Let them have dominion." Once again, they demonstrated that men and women weren't made for defeat. They were created to walk in dominion on this earth.

Our ministry trips often take us to nations across Asia where idol worship is prevalent. A number of years ago, I was ministering in a city which had become a major tourist attraction because of its idol worship. The following week the biggest festival day of the year would take place. They would parade a huge idol through the streets while thousands of people either joined in the parade or prostrated themselves in heathen worship along the parade route as their idol passed by. The idol was made out of plexiglass since it was several stories high and would have been too heavy to move if it had been made out of wood or stone.

As the pastor of the local church was telling me about the events that were scheduled for the following week, we both felt in our spirits that we, as believers in Jesus Christ, should not sit by and let the devil have so much honor and attention in that city. We knew we had power over the devil in this situation.

We were led by the Holy Spirit to go into warfare over the festival which was scheduled the following Saturday. We boldly pulled down the strongholds of the forces of darkness over that city. We boldly declared that in the name of Jesus that parade couldn't take place! The warfare was intense, but we continued in confident obedience, as we were led by the Holy Spirit.

We stopped when we knew the battle had been won in the spirit. We felt in our spirits that some catastrophic event was going to happen which would stop the parade. We were confident the parade would be canceled before the week was out.

The following weekend, I was ministering in another city. When I awakened Sunday morning, I felt impressed to purchase a newspaper to learn what had happened to stop the parade. As I picked up the paper, the headlines told about the terrible tragedy that had happened in the city where we had taken authority over the forces of Satan.

As thousands of pilgrims crowded together in an attempt to get to the parade route, a support gave way and many hundreds were crushed to death. The parade had been canceled.

A couple of years later, I again met with the pastor of the church in that city. He told me that he and a few members of the church had continued to pull down the stronghold of this demonic idol over their city. God had given them specific instructions concerning certain spirits to bind which were part of that idol worship. In obedience to God, he and some of the other Christian leaders in his church continued in warfare over that idol.

Soon they heard the arms of the idol had begun to crack. As they continued to do battle, the arms came crashing down and were broken into hundreds of pieces. As that huge idol continued to disintegrate, the area around the temple where it stands was closed off in an attempt to keep the people from seeing that their idol was literally falling apart.

In the same town, God told the pastor to bind the spirit of the viper. As a result of his obedience, the pit vipers that had been objects of worship for many years left the heathen temple. The priest planted various types of plants and trees in a futile attempt to attract them back.

Because of a revelation of their God-given authority and dominion, the believers in that city are taking their city away from the devil. They are forcibly advancing the kingdom of God, and many are receiving Jesus as their Savior in the city that was once a stronghold of demonic idol worship.

The return of Jesus to this earth is very soon, and Jesus isn't coming back for a weak, defeated bride.

He's coming back for a church that has prevailed against the gates of hell.

The writer of the Book of Hebrews reveals that Jesus is still seated at the right hand of the Father, waiting for something to be fulfilled on this earth before He can return for His bride. We read, *But this Man, after He had offered one sacrifice for sins forever, sat down at the right hand of God, from that time waiting till His enemies are made His footstool* (Hebrews 10:13).

While Jesus is waiting, He is interceding for us. The book of Hebrews records, *Therefore He is also able to save to the uttermost those who come to God through Him, since He ever lives to make intercession for them* (Hebrews 7;25).

At this time, Jesus continues to sit and wait until we, His Church on this earth, discover our restored authority and rise up and forcibly make His enemies — the devil and every demon spirit — to be His footstool on earth. Jesus is waiting until we as His Church, using our God-given, blood-bought, dominion, put Satan under our feet and demonstrate that he and every demon spirit is a defeated foe.

Jesus' work has been completed on this earth. Now He is waiting for us to complete our work. He is waiting for us to fulfill the function for which He created us upon this earth when He said, "Let them have dominion!"

Many are asking, "When will Jesus come back?"

Jesus said, *This gospel of the kingdom will be preached in all the world as a witness to all the nations, and then the end will come* (Matthew 24:14).

Armed with the restored truth of our spiritual authority, the church is going out in greater and greater numbers to take the cities and nations of this world away from the devil.

The church is becoming like the heroes of faith, *Who through faith subdued kingdoms, worked righteousness, obtained promises, stopped the mouths of lions, quenched the violence of fire, escaped the edge of the sword, out of weakness were made strong, became valiant in battle, turned to flight the armies of the aliens (Hebrews 11:33,34).*

As the saints of the Most High, we were destined for dominion from the moment we were created in God's image.

The Word declares, *Then the kingdom and dominion, and the greatness of the kingdoms under the whole heaven, shall be given to the people, the saints of the Most High (Daniel 7:27a).*

God is calling each of us to make a commitment to become part of that mighty army of God who will *put to flight the armies of the aliens.* God is waiting in eager anticipation for us to pull down the strongholds of Satan over our lives, our families, our cities and the nations of the world.

Jesus is waiting until we, like those great heroes of faith, will subdue the kingdoms of the evil one in this world. He is waiting, praying and believing that we will discover that we are

Destined For Dominion!